YOUR GREATEST ADVENTURE

Taking the Next Steps in Your Faith

Jeff Cranston

John Broadbanks Publishing

Endorsements for
Your Greatest Adventure:
Taking the Next Steps in Your Faith

If you're looking for the adventure of your life, then this book is the roadmap, and Jeff Cranston is your guide. Hang on!

Brian Jones, Philadelphia, PA
Author of *Second Guessing God: Hanging On When You Can't See His Plan*

Your Greatest Adventure *is a wonderfully written, practical guide to help light the path for any new believer's journey to deeper faith and spiritual growth. Jeff's experience "walking the walk" and his gift for insightful storytelling help bring to life the most important answers to "now what?" in a relevant and transforming way.*

David Robinson, Bluffton, SC
Colonel, USMC (Ret.)
CEO, Vertical Performance Enterprises

Quick! A dear friend just received Christ—what resource are you going to hand your friend? Now I know the answer! This book will be a faithful guide on life's greatest journey.

Dr. Rob McCleland, Dallas, TX
CEO, LeaderTribe
Past President, The John Maxwell Leadership Foundation

Jeff's book, Your Greatest Adventure, *is a treasure trove of biblical principles and suggested practices for a new Christian's ongoing spiritual formation. He writes with clarity. He advocates a grace-based approach to God's Word and to the behaviors of new believers that will facilitate their growth. His conversational, reader-friendly writing style teems with interesting stories, apt analogies, and quotes from other sources. But this isn't just a book for the new Christian. Its practical content will also serve anyone who is mentoring a new believer or leading a class of recent converts to the faith.*

Terry Powell, Columbia, SC
Faculty Emeritus, Columbia International University

Jeff Cranston has lived, taught, and preached the essential principles of God's Word his entire ministry. I have been privileged to watch him teach, and then lead, thousands of people to personal faith in Jesus. I am thankful that he has now written an effective "tool" which communicates these foundational principles in clear language for new believers as they begin their new lives with Christ.

Carl F. Martin, Jr., Ridgeland, SC
Executive Director, Real Champions Inc.

Some of the most challenging days for a follower of Jesus are in the first few weeks of their new relationship with God. The prevailing question for the new believer is often, "Now what?" Out of his desire to fill this gap, Jeff Cranston has developed a resource that is biblically sound and practically helpful to give new believers the handles they need to live out their faith. I cannot more highly recommend Your Greatest Adventure *to pastors as a resource for their churches and to new believers eager to answer the "Now what?" question.*

Jay Hardwick, Columbia, SC
Associate Executive Director and Chief Strategist
South Carolina Baptist Convention

Every Sunday, I share the gospel with those attending our church. And, every Sunday, I immediately offer a free resource to help a new believer grow in Christ. While I am grateful for the present resources available to me, I have been looking for a resource just like Jeff Cranston has published. To place a book into the hands of someone who has just received Christ (or still seeking to discover Jesus), written by a pastor in the arena of the church every day, is huge for me. Jeff's intent is appreciated and the content is so real and practical. I plan on purchasing a lot of copies of Your Greatest Adventure. *While this book won't do much good sitting on a table in a church foyer, it will do a world of good in the hands of a new believer.*

Thanks, Jeff! With this resource, you are really helping our church's calling to share the gospel and develop new disciples in the 21st Century!

John Hull, Marietta, GA
Lead Pastor, Eastside Baptist Church

John Broadbanks Publishing
Eureka, CA

10 9 8 7 6 5 4 3 2 1

Printed in the United States of America

ISBN: 978-0-9975974-8-6
eISBN: 978-0-9975974-9-3

Cover Design: Andrea Smith
Interior Layout: Marcia Breece
eBook: Marcia Breece

TABLE OF CONTENTS

DEDICATION

Your Greatest Adventure is dedicated to my grandchildren: Callie, Cade, Colt, and Charley (and every other grandchild as the Lord may bless). As they grow up, their spiritual growth comes with my fervent prayers and hope that the gift of God's undeserved grace and the understanding that comes from Jesus will be known by them in all its fullness.

A CONVERT'S FIRST PRAYER

MY FATHER,
  I could never have sought my happiness
    in thy love,
  unless thou had'st first loved me.
Thy Spirit has encouraged me by grace to seek thee,
  has made known to me thy reconciliation in Jesus,
  has taught me to believe it,
  has helped me to take thee for my God
    and portion.
May he grant me to grow in the knowledge
    and experience of thy love,
  and walk in it all the way to glory.
Blessed forever be thy fatherly affection,
  which chose me to be one of thy children
    by faith in Jesus:
I thank thee for giving me the desire to live as such.
In Jesus, my brother, I have my new birth,
  every restraining power,
  every renewing grace.

It is by thy Spirit I call thee Father,
  believe in thee, love thee;
Strengthen me inwardly for every purpose
  of my Christian life;
Let the Spirit continually reveal to me my interest
  in Christ,
    and open to me the riches of thy love in him;
    May he abide in me that I may know my union
      with Jesus,
    and enter into constant fellowship with him;
By thy Spirit may I daily live to thee,
  rejoice in thy love,
    find it the same to me as to thy Son,
    and become rooted and grounded in it
      as a house on rock;
I know but little—
  increase my knowledge of thy love in Jesus,
  keep me pressing forward for clearer discoveries
    of it,
  so that I may find its eternal fullness;
Magnify thy love to me according to its greatness,
  and not according to my deserts or prayers,
  and whatever increase thou givest,
  let it draw out greater love to thee.[1]

—A Puritan Prayer

PREFACE

Congratulations!

By placing your faith in the Lord Jesus Christ, you have made the greatest, wisest, and best decision of your life. And it will pay dividends to you for all eternity.

Now what happens? The answer to that question is the reason I wrote this book. I wanted to place a resource in your hands that you could return to time and again as you progress from taking your first tentative steps as a new believer to further strides leading you deeper into a mature faith.

You are beginning a new life, and there will be a number of changes that will take place in your life. You will need some help, and each chapter has been written with those changes in mind.

I hope this becomes more than another book to you; I hope it will serve as a guide to get you started on the right track as you follow Jesus. As you read, I urge you to take it all in, let these new truths settle into your heart, and then follow through and live it out.

Pastor and author John MacArthur defines spiritual growth as simply matching up your practice with your position. Your position in Christ is secure, held by Him, and perfect. Now, God desires that you walk that out in practice—aligning your behavior with your newfound belief—as He helps and guides you by His Holy Spirit.

Enjoy your greatest adventure!

—Jeff Cranston

BY WAY OF INTRODUCTION

"Very often the only way to get a quality in reality is to start behaving as if you had it already. That is why children's games are so important. They are always pretending to be grown-ups—playing soldiers, playing shop. But all the time, they are hardening their muscles and sharpening their wits, so that the pretense of being grown-ups helps them to grow up in earnest."

—C. S. Lewis[1]

Serving in ministry for more than thirty-five years, I have reveled in being on the front lines of the local church. I have witnessed thousands of people hand their lives over to Jesus Christ, trusting in Him as their Lord and Savior. I have seen with my own eyes the miraculous transaction that takes place when someone crosses from darkness into light, from lies to truth, and from death to life.

And then I watched many of them drift away.

Their glide away from God occurred due to various reasons. Jesus told us this might happen. Sitting in a boat, teaching a multitude of people on shore, He said:

> "Listen! A farmer went out to plant some seeds. As he scattered them across his field, some seeds fell on a footpath, and the birds came and ate them. Other seeds fell on shallow soil with underlying rock. The seeds sprouted quickly because the soil was shallow. But the plants soon wilted under the hot sun, and since they didn't have deep roots, they died. Other seeds fell among thorns that grew up and choked out the tender plants. Still other seeds fell on fertile soil, and they produced a crop that was thirty, sixty, and even a hundred times as much as had been planted! Anyone with ears to hear should listen and understand."[2]

In other words, the gospel will take root in some people; in others, it will not. I believe every word Jesus ever said, but I have to admit that this passage troubles me. Why can't every person who believes remain?

The answers lie within the parable[3] itself and Jesus' explanation of it. He not only shared the parable, He revealed its meaning. Allow me to sum it up: the farmer is the proclaimer of God's truth, the seed is the gospel, and the soil is the human heart.

The footpath represents the hardhearted person: the one who is resistant to the gospel and is not willing to ask questions, delve deeper, and who is disinclined to hear and take it all in. This is the fool, who in the Book of Psalms[4], says there is no God—the one who makes a soul-destroying decision. The birds are representative of Satan who *"comes and snatches away what has been sown in his heart."*[5]

Other seeds fell on shallow soil with underlying rock. This soil was never tilled, never worked. Jesus explains:

> *"As for what was sown on rocky ground, this is the one who hears the word and immediately receives it with joy, yet he has no root in himself, but endures for a while, and when tribulation or persecution arises on account of the word, immediately he falls away."*[6]

Such a clear picture! This person has heard the gospel and exclaimed, "This is the best news ever! Count me in; where do I sign up?" With the receiving of the gospel, however, there must also come a commitment. Without a commitment to Jesus, the person's faith initially sprang up and got off to a good start, but he never counted the cost or considered the gospel anything more than a fire escape from hell.

Christianity is costly. It has cost countless millions their jobs, their loved ones, their reputations, their friendships, and in many cases, their lives. For this person, however, when the pressure came, it was discovered there was no root system.

Next are the seeds that fell among the thorns or weeds. What is this describing? Jesus explains, *". . . this is the one who hears the word, but the cares of the world and the deceitfulness of riches choke the word, and it proves unfruitful."*[7] This individual has heard the Word with a receptive attitude but other things—the riches, snares, and cares of this world—are too compelling for him.

I've seen this happen too many times. The soil looks very good. There was a desperate call to Christ for salvation, but it wasn't all turned over to Him. There was never a complete 180-degree turn, never a full repentance of turning from self and turning fully to Christ. It's the story of the double-minded man the apostle James writes about—the one trying to serve both God and money, for example, but the deceitfulness of materialism and riches was too strong a pull.

The last category of soil is the hopeful part of all of this. *"As for what was sown on good soil, this is the one who hears the word and understands it. He indeed bears fruit and yields, in one case a hundredfold, in another sixty, and in another thirty."*[8]

This is the fruit-bearing life, the life that understands, and having fully repented and turning to Christ, accepts the Word. Dr. Luke, in his retelling of this parable, describes this person as the one, *". . . who hold[s] it fast in an honest and good heart . . ."*[9] That's it. The good soil person hears it, accepts it, holds it, and takes the gospel in. There is a genuine repentance. There's a genuine plowing of the Spirit of God in the heart, killing all those noxious weeds of a former life. And there's some deep soil there instead of a rock bed of selfish resistance. The fruit then follows.

Every Christian will bear some fruit, but not every Christian will produce the same amount of fruit. However, we all produce fruit. That's a distinguishing mark of Christ-followers.

As you hold this book in your hands, it goes with my prayer for you, that the soil of your heart—rich, loamy, and fertile—will always be the soil that produces fruit.

This book is born out of the heart of a mildly frustrated pastor. My frustration has come when I think of those I've known who fell away from their faith, possibly because no one ever took the time to come alongside of them, walking them through the initial phases of their Christian life. It's my hope that this book might do that for you.

Each chapter covers an area of our shared faith that is vitally important. I endeavor to explain it in an understandable manner and provide some applications which might serve to get you on your way.

It is my prayer that as you read this book and begin to understand the theology and concepts of a growing relationship with Jesus Christ, that you will flourish in your newfound faith and encourage others to join you in following Him.

> *Father of mercies, we have need*
> *Of Thy preparing grace;*
> *Let the same Hand that gives the seed*
> *Provide a fruitful place!*[10]

—Jeff Cranston

CHAPTER ONE

What Just Happened?

> *"A new birth is [the] most sweeping . . . process conceivable. It is, in fact, more than a change, it is a creation . . . a new life must be received and no improving the present life will suffice in its place."*
> —*C. H. Spurgeon*[1]

What's your favorite television show category? Is it tried-and-true Hallmark Christmas movies? Or could it be mysteries or dramas or maybe even shows that teach you how to cook? If you're thinking makeover TV shows, you've chosen a popular category. There are so many addictive makeover shows that a lot of us love to binge-watch.

This category of TV show includes home, lifestyle, and fashion makeovers. Some shows focus on specific kinds of makeovers, while others focus on the interior transformation as much as the exterior. People watch because they enjoy agreeing or disagreeing with the stylistic choices of the makeover artists. Yet, fans are engrossed with the entire show as much as the big reveal at the end. Virtually every one of these shows, however, focus on taking something old, worn down, tired, and just plain ugly, and then making it look better.

You have recently entered into a new relationship with Jesus—a makeover of sorts. God, however, does not just give you a new makeover—updating the old in order to make the existing look better—He makes you completely new! The Bible says that you have been born again, and as such, the Scriptures say that you are a new creation.

A New You

One of my favorite Bible verses is found in the apostle Paul's second letter to the Christians who lived in Corinth, a city in Greece. To these Christ-followers, many of them new to the Christian faith, Paul wrote: "*Therefore if anyone is in Christ, he is a new creature; the old things passed away; behold, new things have come.*"[2] The term, "in Christ" means that you now are experiencing a union with Christ—that His Spirit is now residing within you. Being a new creation means that you are something which has never before existed!

This reminds me of a story about London businessman Lindsay Clegg, who was selling a warehouse property. The building had sat empty for months and needed repairs. Vandals had damaged the doors, smashed the windows, and strewn trash around the interior. As Clegg showed a prospective buyer the property, he took pains to say that he would replace the broken windows, bring in a crew to correct any structural damage, and clean out the garbage. "Forget about the repairs," the buyer said. "When I buy this place, I'm going to build something completely different. I don't want the building; I want the site."[3]

Compared with the renovation God has in mind, our efforts to improve our own lives are as trivial as sweeping a warehouse slated for the wrecking ball. When we become God's, our old life is over. He makes all things new. All He wants is the site and the permission to build.

You are no longer the same; you are different. You have been changed! Not as an imitation to look more like Christ but rather a conversion in order to be like Christ. Change has occurred at the very core of your being. It's a change that has altered your essence. *"No longer I but Christ lives within,"*[4] the Bible teaches us. You are a brand-new person!

We know that the old life has gone, and a new life burgeons. Your old life is all of the things which were once true of you in your sinful state. These were passed down from our first father, Adam. You remember Adam and Eve. Through them, sin entered our world. You were once "in Adam." You are now "in Christ." Whereas you formerly identified with Adam, you now identify with Jesus. At the moment of your salvation, a number of things happened. One of those things is that you became a new creation—a person commonly referred to as a Christian.

A New Heart

There is a world-renowned heart clinic where I live. Patients check into it from all over the globe. The clinic has improved the quality of life for thousands of heart patients. When someone comes to them with a heart issue, after a thorough examination, that patient may be presented with a number of potential treatments. Sometimes, however, there is only one best option: a heart transplant.

That's an analogy for the spiritual heart within. Our real problem is a heart problem. We're born spiritually dead without any spark of the Divine within. A transplant was needed!

That transplant occurred the moment you became a Christian. When you prayed, asking Christ to come into your life as your Lord and Savior, an exchange took place: your old, evil heart was exchanged for a new heart of righteousness in Christ. The prophet Ezekiel put it like this: *"Moreover, I will give you a new heart and put a new spirit within you; and I will remove the heart of stone from your flesh and give you a heart of flesh."*[5]

The words "heart" and "spirit" are often synonymous in the Bible. This verse means that to have a new heart is to have a new spirit. This is something only God can do. We cannot do it to ourselves. The spirit of lying deception has been replaced by God's spirit of truth.

Jesus wants to accomplish so much in and through you. In order for that to take place, it will be very helpful for you to understand as much as you can about what all of this means. You can start by acknowledging that you, under your own power, cannot accomplish anything of the Spirit. It's all up to God!

A New Realization

Take a moment and ponder the momentous change God has made in you. The Bible says you now have been given a new nature. There has been a conversion from your old self and old ways to a new self and new ways. This conversion or change has occurred within and is something which God has brought. The source of all change—God Himself—has done this. Christ now lives within you, and He will do all the work that has happened, is happening now, and will happen in your future.

Your heavenly Father has placed His Holy Spirit within you. He is the change agent in your life now. Life is no longer about you cleaning up your act; it is the Holy Spirit who is at work in your life. From this moment on, decide to stop trying, struggling, seeking to improve yourself, and instead yield to God's Spirit. All of our human efforts result in nothing but failure if you are trying to please God and court His favor. The sooner we come to that realization, the better. Stop trusting in the flesh and start trusting wholly in Christ. The flesh will always fail us; Jesus never will.

A New Identity

When Victor Serebriakoff was fifteen, his teacher told him he would never finish school and that he should drop out and learn a trade. Victor took the teacher's advice, dropped out of school, and for the next seventeen years, he moved from town to town doing a variety of odd jobs. His teacher told him he was ignorant and would never succeed when it came to using his brain, and Victor entered his adult years firmly believing that.

Then suddenly, when he was thirty-two, an amazing transformation took place. Victor underwent an evaluative process which discovered that he had an I.Q. of 161! Guess what happened? That's right: Victor started acting like a genius—he wrote books, secured patents, and became a successful businessman. Perhaps most significantly, Victor Serebriakoff, the high school dropout, turned itinerant handyman, was elected chairman of the International Mensa Society. To be accepted to Mensa, a person must have an I.Q. in the top 2 percent of the population.[6]

What made the difference for Victor? Did he suddenly become exponentially intelligent at his thirty-second birthday party? No. What changed was the way he saw himself.

For all of your life, up until your decision to follow Jesus Christ, you have lived beneath the privileges God had for you. At the moment of your conversion, a major paradigm shift occurred. The old is gone; the new has come! You now have a new position, new possession, and new potential—all found in Christ.

If you take a look in the mirror you may notice that not much, if anything, has changed. You are still you in the mirror. When we take an inside look, however, it's not the same old, same old anymore! What used to be there is gone, and things that are completely new are now in place.

Perhaps I can explain. Here in the South, we love our sweet iced tea. If you ever want a chuckle, watch what happens when someone craving a sweet tea on a sweltering summer day is accidently brought unsweet tea by the restaurant server. Such a face you will seldom see! A grimacing, shocked visage quickly gives way to a vocal aspersion along the lines of, "Aaaggghhhh!!!! What is this? This is not sweet tea! How could anyone in their right mind drink this?!" These words are also usually accompanied by physical gyrations that do not settle down until another tea glass is delivered, and after a tentative first sip, a rapturous exclamation of satisfaction is uttered. All is right with the world again.

What has taken place during the saga of the sweet tea episode? The right drink has been ordered. The server brought it in a tea glass. It looked exactly like sweet tea. The surprise came because the contents had changed—and that made all of the difference.

Similarly, as a new creature—a new creation in Christ—your contents have changed. Inwardly, you are radically different than you were prior to placing your complete trust and faith in Jesus Christ to save and forgive you. The difference in you now is not physical, it is spiritual—not external, but internal. You have lost your old life.

Jesus taught us about this when He said, *"The person who tries to preserve his life will lose it, but the person who loses his life for me will preserve it."*[7] The Christian no longer looks within for identity or success or to other people. When that happens, the person inwardly comes up short. Only when you lose what you perceive to be life, will you ever find true life and true identity. We find what deeply and really matters only in Jesus Christ.

Once I have received Jesus as Lord and Savior, I then begin to identify with Him in His life, death, burial, and resurrection. At the moment of conversion, you were made one with Him. You now have a brand-new identity—in Christ alone.

God, through the power of the Holy Spirit, is already beginning to make you into the likeness of Christ. While you retain your personality and individuality, you gain a whole new identity.

Now What?

For the individual whose life has been changed by Jesus one of the earliest inclinations is to begin living for Him. You have a zeal within that you have never known before—a zeal to live and honor God. Follow up on that. Don't sit idly by. Refuse to become passive. Paul tells us as much when he writes, "*But now finish doing it also, so that just as there was the readiness to desire it, so there may be also the completion of it by your ability.*"[8]

While remembering that there is nothing you can do to be accepted by God—Jesus has secured God's acceptance of you because of the Cross—you can begin living for Him. You are now free and empowered toward a deep level of divine activity in your life. You are free to do what God has made you to do. You are free to become the person He wants you to become.

The following chapters will hopefully get you on your way. Let's get started!

CHAPTER TWO

Assurance:

How to Know That You Know

When my two oldest daughters were in elementary school, my wife Darlene and I took Tiff and Lauren to see the play, *Anne of Green Gables.*[1] Anne was an orphan girl brought out to live at a homestead on Canada's Prince Edward Island called Green Gables. Matthew Cuthbert, and his sister, Marilla, thought they were getting a boy to help with the farm chores. Anne, seeing the beauty of the farm, immediately fell in love with her new surroundings. She made every attempt to persuade the family to allow her to stay.

She pleaded, she cajoled, she begged, and she promised. She would make up her bed, help cook, sweep the rugs, and wash and dry the dishes. She had been kicked out of so many homes since her parents had died that she was going to hold on to this one by being good and obedient. All the while in the back of her mind were the fears and doubts that Matthew and Marilla would not let her permanently stay with them.

Many times, we're a lot like Anne, aren't we? "Am I really good enough for God?" "Will He really let me into His heaven?" "Have I done all that I need to do in order to be accepted by Him?" It is His business and His desire for each of His children to have assurance of his or her salvation. God's job in the universe is not to go around saying to all men and women everywhere, "Trust Me," and then make us wonder for the rest of our lives if we really did trust Him. He does not say, "I'll save you," only to pull a cosmic prank and not really save us. So, how do you know that you know Him? Why do you doubt? Let's examine some common causes for doubt and lack of assurance.

You may have doubts because you have never actually given your life to Christ.

What can you do about that? The apostle Paul pens:

> *Test yourselves to make sure you are solid in the faith. Don't drift along taking everything for granted. Give yourselves regular checkups. You need firsthand evidence, not mere hearsay, that Jesus Christ is in you. Test it out. If you fail the test, do something about it.*[2]

The Bible also says, "*But land that produces thorns and thistles is worthless and is in danger of being cursed. In the end it will be burned.*"[3]

"Fail the test," and being in "danger of being cursed" are all the same Greek word. Our English word, *reprobate*, sums up both of these terms. Examine yourself right now.

Ask yourself these questions about past decisions:

- Was my decision to follow Christ my own, or did I make it to please someone else?
- Was I aware, at that time, I was a sinner?
- Was I sorry—truly sorry—for my sins?
- Did I understand that Jesus Christ died to pay the penalty for my sins?
- Did I repent of my sins and ask God to forgive me?
- Did I willingly invite Jesus Christ into my heart to be my Savior and Lord?

Settle the matter, once and for all—now.

If you answered yes to the previous questions, then you need to take God at His Word, thank Him for the great salvation He has given you, and go about making yourself useful in His service. God has preserved His precious book, the Bible, down through the centuries so that we may have something upon which to rest our faith. God has spoken through this written revelation, and He tells us that to believe on the name of His Son is to know that we have eternal life.

The great nineteenth-century evangelist, D. L. Moody, once remarked, "I believe hundreds of Christians have not got the assurance of salvation just because they are not willing to take God at His Word."

If you cannot answer yes to those questions, you need to re-evaluate your life and where you stand with the Lord Jesus Christ. He came into this world to pay the complete price for your sins, and He paid with His life. He now offers you the gift of eternal life. What will you do with Jesus right now?

You might have doubts because you think you may have lost your salvation.

This raises some very important questions. "Can a saved person be lost again?" "Can you know for sure that you are saved before you die, or must you wait until you stand before God in eternity to find out?"

Some say you can be lost again after Christ has saved you. The Bible says otherwise. John, the beloved disciple, records the words of Jesus:

> "My sheep listen to my voice; I know them, and they follow me. I give them eternal life, and they will never perish. No one will snatch them away from me, for my Father has given them to me, and he is more powerful than anyone else. No one can snatch them from the Father's hand."[4]

Some say you only have the prospect of eternal life here, but you cannot be assured of it until after you die; but the Bible says you can know. Jesus said, *"Very truly I tell you, whoever hears my word and believes him who sent me has eternal life and will not be judged but has crossed over from death to life."*[5]

In his book, *Failure Is Not an Option*, former aerospace engineer and NASA flight director, Gene Kranz wrote, "When reporters asked [astronaut Alan] Shepard what he thought about as he sat atop the Redstone rocket, waiting for liftoff, he had replied, 'The fact that every part of this ship was built by the lowest bidder.'"[6]

The work of salvation did not go to the lowest bidder but was performed by a loving act by your infinite God. There will never be a deficiency in His work. Our salvation is as sure as He is! And when you have it, you have it for all of eternity; when you have it, you have it right now. No ifs, ands, or buts!

Some say you must wait until you stand before God to really know whether or not you are saved. The Bible says you can know right now. The Bible says:

> *So, whoever has the Son, has life; whoever rejects the Son, rejects life. My purpose in writing is simply this: that you who believe in God's Son will know beyond the shadow of a doubt that you have eternal life, the reality and not the illusion.*[7]

There's a story about an elementary school boy who had given his life to Jesus. Before going to bed one night he read a Scripture text his pastor had given him. They were the same verses as above. "I have life," he said, "for I have received the Son." A voice seemed to say from somewhere underneath the bed, "No, you haven't." "Yes, I have," he replied. "No, you haven't," the voice insisted. And so, the argument went back and forth. Finally, Johnny got up, turned on the light, and found the text. He read it aloud, "Whoever has the Son has life . . ." Again, he seemed to hear the voice saying, "No, you don't." Taking his open Bible, he pushed it under the bed and said, "There you are. Read it for yourself!"

That's how Christ dealt with the enemy in the wilderness. When Satan puts doubts in your mind, hit him with the Word of God. When God says you are His child, that means you are His child, no matter what the devil says.

You may have doubts because you are allowing sinful acts, habits, or thoughts a protected place in your life, and your fellowship with God is broken. In the Psalms, King David said, *"If I had been cozy with evil, the Lord would never have listened."*[8]

Broken fellowship with the Lord almost makes us feel as we felt before we knew Him: alone, empty, and guilty. Why does God allow this to happen? *So that we will return to Him.* Once you deal with the sin problem in your life—if there is one—the doubts will be dispelled.

God wants you to live a clean and surrendered life before Him on a daily basis. Questions and doubts can be beneficial: they can lead us to a place of absolute dependence upon God.

You may be struggling with doubts because you are resisting God's will for your life.

Perhaps God is calling you to special service—teacher, preacher, or missionary—and you are resisting His call. Perhaps He is calling you to a sense of being totally sold out to Him, and you are resisting and refusing. Perhaps God is asking for a blank sheet of paper from you that He wants to fill in, and you are finding yourself reluctant and fearful. If this is the case, allow the Word of God to speak to your heart through these verses:

> *. . . because God is working in you to help you want to do and be able to do what pleases him.*[9]

> *Does not the potter have the right to make out of the same lump of clay some pottery for special purposes and some for common use?*[10]

Trust in the Lord with all your heart and lean not on your own understanding; in all your ways submit to him and he will make your paths straight.[11]

How Can I Know if I am God's Child?

The Bible says, *"Now we look inside, and what we see is that anyone united with the Messiah gets a fresh start, is created new. The old life is gone; a new life burgeons! Look at it!"*[12]

The key word here is *new*! When Christ comes into your life, He brings the *new* with Him! All things become new. Our new life in Christ is manifested in certain, major areas. Let's look at just a few:

You will gain a new knowledge that God is your heavenly Father.

Matthew 11:27 declares that no one can know the Father except the Son and those to whom the Son will reveal Him.[13] It is one thing to know about God as anyone can know about Him; it is something else to know God as the Son reveals Him. The Bible teaches us, *"And eternal life is this: to know you, the only true God, and Jesus Christ whom you have sent."*[14] Fellowship with God the Father and Jesus, His Son, is known only by those who *"walk in the light,"* according to 1 John 1:7. A normal Christian experience includes a personal appreciation for the Fatherhood of God.

You will experience a new reality in prayer, a confirming experience that leads to assurance.

Prayer assumes a large role in the life of the believer. It increasingly becomes our most vital resource. Praying according to the Spirit should become the norm for every follower of Christ. By the indwelling Spirit we offer praise and thanksgiving; by the Spirit we are enabled to pray according to the will of God. Since Christ's ministry here on earth and in heaven is one so vitally linked with prayer, it will be normal in your life to be moved to prayer. Prayer may have never been a normal part of your life before. Since Jesus has come into your life, expect some changes in this area!

You will sense a new ability to understand the Scriptures.

In John 16:12-15, Christ promises that God's children will understand the things of God through the Holy Spirit and of things to come. On the Emmaus road, Christ opened the Word to His hearers and opened their hearts to Scripture. The Bible relates to us that the two disciples, "*. . . began telling each other how their hearts had felt strangely warm as he talked with them and explained the Scriptures during the walk down the road.*"[15]

Such an experience, though so wonderful, is not designed for super spiritual, holier-than-thou saints; it is meant to be the normal experience for all followers of Christ everywhere—of all those who are right with God. The Bible says, "*But as his anointing teaches you about all things and as that anointing is real, not counterfeit— just as it has taught you, remain in him.*"[16] Understanding things of the Spirit that you have never before understood is a result of salvation. This comes because Christ lives in you!

You will experience a new sense of the wickedness of sin.

This will be, in increasing measure, a normal experience for you. The Word of God, the indwelling Holy Spirit, and the indwelling Christ implants within you ideals and values that are God's.

Lord Byron, one of England's most famous poets, spent his entire life in a mad search for pleasure. He tried his best to live it up. And yet in despair he wrote:

> The thorns I have reaped are from the tree I
> have planted.
> They have torn me and I bleed.
> I should have known what fruit would spring
> From such a tree.[17]

When you understand sin's rapacity and all of its heinous attachments, you understand fully that nothing you can do will be enough to save you. You fully realize and sense your need for a Savior.

The following story reminds us of this truth: A Christian fellow worked in a cabinet shop with another man who was not a believer. This second cabinetmaker was brilliant in his work, yet he felt very strongly that he had to do something to earn his salvation. The Christian coworker spent months speaking to him about this issue but just could not convince him otherwise.

One day the Christian cabinetmaker admired a piece of work the man had finished. With a hint of sanctified mischief in his eyes, he picked up a wood plane and said, "I'm going to see if I can ease off this corner and put a finishing touch on it." At this, the cabinetmaker cried out, "Man alive! Don't do that! It's a finished piece!"

The Christian said, "That's what I've been trying to tell you for the last few months. The work of Christ for your salvation is a finished work. You can't add anything to it. All you have to do is accept it." The man saw the point and decided for Christ then and there.

You will have a new love for those who do not yet know Christ.

Jesus died for the sins of all persons everywhere. People are seen by God as creatures sorely needing redemption—redemption that only Christ can provide. For them he was even willing to be "cursed," according to Romans 9:1-3. As a result of Christ's divine presence within you, there comes a divine compassion that is the compassion of Christ. This passion for those without Him will become a normal experience for you if you know Christ as your Lord and Savior.

You will gain a new love for fellow believers.

Someone penned the following humorous poem:

> *To dwell up above with the saints that we love,*
> *Oh, how that will be glory.*
> *But to dwell here below with the saints that we know,*
> *Man, that's another story!*

The litmus test for personal salvation is a love for your new family members who are also in Christ. The Bible says, *"We know we have left death and have come into life because we love each other. Whoever does not love is still dead."*[18] This is reasonable, since by the regenerating work of the Holy Spirit, we are brought into a new kinship in the household and the family of God. It is here that the true Fatherhood of God and the brotherhood of man is manifest. The fact that the divine presence and Spirit of Christ indwells me and indwells you relates us in vital ways.

That explains how you can cross oceans, time zones, and cultures and find intimate fellowship with those within the same body of Christ. Our love for one another is the insignia of true discipleship. This holy affection for fellow believers is the normal experience for you when you are born again.

Questions and Doubts

Are you finding your inward voice sounding something like the following? "I know that I am a sinner. There is no question about that. I know that all the good works that I can do will never get me to heaven. Therefore, I have come to Christ many, many times receiving Him into my heart. I have asked Christ into my life over and over and over again. Every Sunday it is difficult for me to give thanks and praise to God because I am constantly wondering about this gnawing, aching question: Am I really saved? How can I praise Him if I don't know whether or not I am saved? It's so frustrating and, quite honestly, there are times when I feel like giving up on God and church and just walking away."

May I remind you of something? You are in good company. Those closest to Jesus Christ often had questions and doubts in their minds.

Peter kept stumbling again and again. He cut off the soldier's ear in the garden when Jesus was arrested; he denied Christ three times—one time, even cursing at a servant girl. He failed; he questioned; he doubted. He experienced fluctuating emotions. Yet, Jesus, when He appeared to the disciples, re-affirmed Peter by telling Him, "*Shepherd my sheep.*"[19]

Thomas forcibly stated that he would not believe in Jesus' resurrection until he could see Him and touch the wounds in His hand and sides. Jesus showed up, spoke personally to Thomas, engendering this response from Thomas: "*My Lord and my God!*"[20]

John the Baptist sent his disciples to inquire of Jesus: "*Are you the One we've been expecting, or are we still waiting?*"[21]

It is imperative to differentiate between a doubt and a question. Doubt asks, "Is this thing true?" A question looks for answers to explain what is true in a given situation. For example, Job did not doubt God or doubt God's existence. He questioned how God and his circumstances fit into the present paradigm of his life.

If you are struggling in any of these areas, find a godly friend to pray with you through this shadowy night of your soul. Examine yourself and check out what is "new" to you. And remember: Christ saw those closest to Him go through excruciating times of questioning.

Remember Anne of Green Gables? At the end of her story, she moved to a place called Avonlea. She was the most secure and confident young woman one could ever hope to find. She was holding a very fine teaching position at a girls academy and was the toast of the town. She was comfortable with who she was. What happened to the insecure, pigtailed, red-haired orphan girl?

Assurance had been grafted into her life, assurance that Matthew and Marilla would not kick her out of their home and that they would love Anne for who she was.

We're like that. Maybe right now you're working very hard at being obedient because you don't have assurance. What can you do to have assurance?

Persevere! Hold on! Pretty soon, you will be so tired of trying to do it all on your own, so tired of holding on that your white knuckles will let go, and at that moment you will make the wonderful discovery that God was holding you the whole time. You will know that you know that you know Him.

CHAPTER THREE

Baptism:
The Waters of Obedience

Shortly after a recent seminary graduate had assumed his first pastorate, he and his wife went to visit his family one Saturday. His mother sensed that her daughter-in-law was unhappy, but not wanting to meddle, she pretended not to notice. As they were leaving, she heard her daughter-in-law say, "All right, we can go by the church and you can pretend baptizing me just one more time. But remember this: when you conduct your first funeral, you are not going to practice burying me!"

Many pastors can tell humorous stories about baptisms. It seems that if Murphy's Law[1] applies to anything, it applies to baptisms. I know of one minister who was assisting a just-baptized believer out of the water, when the microphone fell from its stand into the baptismal pool! He came through his electrically charged experience relatively unscathed, but only after being carried out of the church service on a stretcher to a waiting ambulance and the emergency room!

Here's another humorous, but less electrifying story: In March 1888, *The Memphis Daily Avalanche* newspaper printed the following story: "A precocious four-year-old at Englewood has recently attended several baptismal services in the church and was greatly impressed thereby. The other day she was observed by her mother putting her doll through the form of baptism she had seen practiced. She said: 'I now baptize you in the name of the Father, and of the Son, and in the hole you go!'"

Yes, there are many stories regarding baptisms that bring a chuckle, but baptism is a very solemn, serious ordinance of the Church of Jesus Christ. We read of baptisms all throughout Scripture. We find . . .

the baptism of Moses
the baptism of John
the baptism of Jesus
the baptism of the Cross
the baptism of the Holy Spirit
the baptism of judgment
and, the baptism of believers.

This chapter focuses on the baptism of believers. Let's begin by asking the question, "What does baptism mean?"

The Meaning of Baptism

Jesus says:

> *"All authority in heaven and on earth has been given to me. Therefore go and make disciples of all nations, baptizing them in the name of the Father and of the Son and of the Holy Spirit, and teaching them to obey everything I have commanded you. And surely I am with you always, to the very end of the age."*[2]

The Life Application Study Bible makes this note: "The disciples were to baptize people because baptism unites a believer with Jesus Christ in his or her death to sin and resurrection to new life. *Baptism symbolizes submission to Christ,* a willingness to live God's way, and identification with God's covenant people" (italics mine).[3] The only response a yielded Christian is to have to Christ is one of total obedience. What Jesus says, we are to do. He said, "*If you love Me, you will keep My commandments.*"[4]

You may have grown up with adults telling you not to smoke because "it will stunt your growth." That may or may not be true, but disobedience to Christ does stunt your growth—your spiritual growth. God will not reveal more of His will to us until we live at a point of obedience. Jesus says, *"Anyone who chooses to do the will of God will find out whether my teaching comes from God or whether I speak on my own."*[5] In the Old Testament, Samuel declared, *". . . to obey is better than sacrifice . . ."*[6]

There is no substitute for obedience. The Bible says, *"For whoever keeps the whole law and yet stumbles in one point, he has become guilty of all."*[7]

There are a number of reasons why we obey God:

Fear: We obey because we have to, and we're afraid of what God might do to us if we disobey Him.

Reward: We obey God because we might get something out of it.

Love: We simply obey because we love Christ and want to please Him. It is the response God is looking for from us.

A well-known preacher had a brother who was a famous physician. One day a woman, wishing to speak with the minister but not being sure if the man she was about to address was the preacher or the physician, asked, "Are you the doctor who preaches or the doctor who practices?" The words were like a goad to the man of God, stirring his conscience. From that moment on, he lived to not only hear the Word of God and speak it, but also to do it. Baptism is the fruit of obedience based not upon our fear of the Lord, nor our desire to receive something good from Him; rather, it stems from our love for Him.

Our Oneness with Christ

Baptism expresses our *oneness* with Christ in death and burial. In baptism, we show outwardly that we were crucified, judicially, with Christ 2,000 years ago; therefore, in Christ we are dead to sin and self. Experientially, the Holy Spirit makes that real to us.

We are also *buried* with Christ. What is dead must be buried and put out of sight. And if sin and self have been buried, then you and I have no right to go and visit the cemetery and dig up old bones, representing our flesh, which will then paralyze our spiritual walk.

Additionally, we have a oneness with Christ in the *resurrection*. The only grounds on which the Holy Spirit releases the resurrection life of Jesus, in and through us, is when we have accepted, by faith, our place in death and burial.

Paul may have had this typology in mind in Colossians 3 when he uses "take off/put on" terminology. This terminology found a literal parallel in the first-century baptismal practice, where candidates approached the waters wearing old clothes. The old clothes were stripped off as those being baptized entered the waters, and on surfacing, they put on new clothes. The old clothes represented the old life, while the new clothes characterized the new sphere of life and its accompanying behavior changes.

Our Offering for Christ

Baptism is a beautiful figure of a life yielded to another. The person being baptized hands himself over to the one who baptizes. This symbolizes the offering of ourselves to Christ. It must be a complete sacrifice, total obedience, and a public demonstration of our total dedication to Christ without reserve—body, soul, and spirit.

J. Wilbur Chapman, a great American evangelist, had the privilege of traveling to England to preach. While there, he was accorded a visit with General William Booth, the founder of The Salvation Army, who was past eighty years of age at that time. Chapman asked Booth if he would disclose to him the secret of his success.

He hesitated for a second, and I saw the tears come into his eyes and steal down his cheeks,

*and then he said, "I will tell you the secret.
God has had all there was of me. There have
been men with greater brains than I; men
with greater opportunities; but from the day
I got the poor of London on my heart and
the vision of what Jesus Christ could do with
the poor of London, I made up my mind that
God would have all of William Booth that
there was. And if there is anything of power
in The Salvation Army today, it is because
God has all the adoration of my heart, all
the powers of my will, and all the influence
of my life."*[8]

The greatness of the power in our lives originates
from the measure of our surrender. Baptism is our obedience to Christ, our oneness with Christ, and our offering
to Christ.

The Implications of Baptism

When we are baptized, we are publicly confessing two
things: our acceptance of Christ as our Savior and our allegiance to Christ as our Lord.

Our acceptance of Christ as Savior

The Bible says, *"And then he told them, 'Go into all
the world and preach the Good News to everyone. Anyone
who believes and is baptized will be saved. But anyone who
refuses to believe will be condemned.'"*[9]

Our salvation is dependent upon believing, not on
baptism. Baptism is the outward expression of the inward transaction made between you and the Lord. The

repentant thief on the cross believed and was taken to paradise by the Lord who saved him, but he was not baptized. Baptism is the public confession of having received Jesus Christ as Savior. It is not a means of salvation—nor is it necessary for salvation.

Paul says that he was sent, not to baptize, but to preach the gospel—not with words of human wisdom, lest the cross of Christ be emptied of its power. And to what gospel was Paul referring? In the Bible, he tells us, *"The first thing I did was place before you what was placed so emphatically before me: that the Messiah died for our sins, exactly as Scripture tells it . . ."*[10]

Again, the gospel is not the cross of Christ, His atonement, and sacrifice, plus baptism. Salvation comes through Christ and by Christ alone. *"There is salvation in no one else! God has given no other name under heaven by which we must be saved."*[11] And not only no other name— no other anything—baptism included.

Allegiance to Christ as Lord

"Therefore go and make disciples of all the nations, baptizing them . . ."[12] Where there is discipleship, there is lordship. There is no such thing as a disciple without a master.

At baptism we make known the fact that we have received Christ as Savior; we show to angels, people, principalities, and powers that we have acknowledged Christ as Sovereign. The Lord Jesus is looking for men and women who will follow Him with their whole hearts—disciples— not just names on church rolls or on decision cards. He's looking for those who will own Him as Lord and Master.

The Rev. John Stanger labored throughout his adult life as a pastor and theologian in the hamlet of Bessels Green, Kent, in southeastern England. The eighteenth-century minister founded the Bessels Green Baptist Church in 1769, a congregation still alive and well. Behind his life of service is a covenant with God, which he wrote and ratified each year until his death. Read beyond the formality in the language and catch his heart. He wrote in part:

> *This day do I, with the utmost solemnity, surrender myself to Thee. I renounce all former lords that have had dominion over me, and I consecrate to Thee all that I have: the faculties of my mind, the members of my body, my worldly possessions, my time, and my influence over others; to be all used entirely for Thy glory, and resolutely employed in obedience to Thy commands . . . To Thee I leave the management of all events, and say without reserve, "Not my will, but Thine, be done."*[13]

The Method of Baptism

The word *baptism* comes from the Greek word *baptizmo* meaning "to dip; or to make fully wet." It was used by the Greeks when referring to the dyeing of a garment or when drawing water from a bowl by dipping a cup into it.

As we have said, baptism signifies the death, burial, and resurrection of our Lord. If we fail to see those acts—death is down—immersion; burial is under—submersion; resurrection is out—emergence—then baptism loses its significance.

Two outstanding examples of the verb *baptizmo* are the baptism of Jesus Christ in the Jordan River and the baptism of the Ethiopian by Philip. Both the Ethiopian and Philip *"went down into the water . . . [and] came up out of the water."*[14] Total immersion was the mode of baptism in the New Testament and best signifies the death, burial, and resurrection of Jesus Christ.

While I hold firmly to the belief that baptism in the New Testament was by immersion, always following belief in Jesus as Savior and Lord, it is perhaps good to acknowledge that many wonderful Christian people hold a differing viewpoint on the mode of baptism. Namely, there are many who love Jesus and practice baptism in different ways, primarily pouring or sprinkling, often with infants.

There has been much debate within the Protestant church for centuries over this issue as to the meaning and method of baptism. While it is a disputable matter, and a consequential one, it is not one worth breaking fellowship over.

Since baptism is not necessary for salvation, followers of Jesus can agree to disagree and still enjoy fellowship with one another as brothers and sisters in the faith. Baptism is a very important issue, and therefore, believing Christians may choose to worship at different churches because of it. And that's okay! For example, a proponent of infant baptism will not likely worship at a Baptist church nor will a proponent of immersion baptism worship at a Presbyterian church.

This should never be an issue that divides the church or severs a friendship or a family relationship. The methodology of how to baptize isn't a position to call a person to repent over; adhering to one way or another isn't sinful. Instead, we can allow an issue like baptism to lead us into healthy conversations with fellow believers in love, truth, and unity as we explain our position and seek to better understand theirs.

The Recipients of Baptism

Baptism is to be received by those who have heard and received the gospel. The Bible says, *"Anyone who believes and is baptized will be saved . . ."*[15] Baptism does not mean regeneration or the forgiveness of sin; it states the fact of an event that has already transpired beforehand. It is the outward sign of an inner reality. Believing *always* comes *before* baptism in the Bible!

Philip taught the Ethiopian man the deeper truths of the Word of God. After the explanation of the gospel message, the man believed. He cried out, *"Look, here is water. What can stand in the way of my being baptized?"*[16] Then he was baptized. Baptism always follows belief.

Baptism is also for those who have repented. Repentance is twofold: it is turning away from sin and turning instead to serve God. The apostle Peter said, *"Change your life. Turn to God and be baptized, each of you, in the name of Jesus Christ . . ."*[17]

We don't like repentance. It makes us uncomfortable; it requires us to admit that what we are doing or have done is wrong. We're like the little fellow who got his hand stuck inside of an expensive vase. His parents applied soapsuds and cooking oil, every slippery substance they could think of, in hopes of sliding his hand out of that vase. When they seemed ready to break the vase as the only way to release the little fellow's hand, the frightened boy asked, "Would it help if I let go of the quarter I am holding?" We want to hold on to the sin that so easily entangles us.

Many years ago, a major American company had trouble keeping employees working in its assembly plant in Panama. The laborers lived in a very simple economy and gained most of their earthly goods by trading and bartering. The company, however, paid them each week in cash. Since the average employee had more cash after a week's work than he had ever seen, he would periodically quit working, satisfied with what he had made.

What was the solution? Company executives gave all of its employees a Sears catalogue. No one quit working then, because they all wanted the previously undreamt-of things they saw in that book.

Followers of Christ are people who look at what the world offers and choose Christ instead.

Someone once said, "Noah's message from the door of the Ark was not, *'Something good is going to happen to you!'* Amos was not confronted by the high priest of Israel for proclaiming, *'Confession is possession!'* Jeremiah was not put into the pit for preaching, *'I'm OK, you're OK.'* Daniel was not put into the lion's den for telling people, *'Possibility thinking will move mountains!'* John the Baptist was not beheaded because he preached, *'Smile! God loves you!'* The two prophets, of which the Book of Revelation tells us, will not be killed for preaching, *'God is in His heaven and all is right with the world.'"*

If these were not their messages, then what message did they herald? What was the simple message of all these men of God? Simple. One word: *"Repent."* Those who have repented of their sins before almighty God are eligible to be baptized.

Baptism is also for those who have received the Holy Spirit. *"Do I hear any objections to baptizing these friends with water? They've received the Holy Spirit exactly as we did."*[18] Paul teaches us, *"The Spirit himself testifies with our spirit that we are God's children."*[19] By the fact of conversion, we possess the Holy Spirit of God.

Dr. A. J. Gordon, one of the founders of the Gordon-Conwell Theological Seminary in Massachusetts, told of being out for a walk and looking across a field at a house. There beside the house was what looked like a man pumping furiously at one of those old hand pumps for water. As he watched, this fellow seemed to pump at a tremendous rate, tirelessly, pumping on and on, up and down, without ever slowing, much less stopping.

It was such a remarkable sight that Gordon began to walk closer. As he got nearer to the man, he realized it was not a man at all, but a wooden figure painted to look like a man. The arm that was pumping so furiously was hinged at the elbow and the hand was wired to the pump handle. The water was pouring forth, but not because the figure of the man was pumping it. It was an artesian well, and the water was pumping the man!

When you see a man or woman who is at work for God and producing results, recognize that it is the Holy Spirit working through that person and not the person's efforts that are giving the results. All we have to do is to keep our hand on the handle.

When we're filled by the Holy Spirit, we can and should follow Christ's example through the waters of obedience—baptism. It is not, "I'll wait until I get baptized, then I can receive the Holy Spirit." As Peter points out in Acts 10, the believers have already received the Holy

Spirit; what is hindering them from being baptized?

Rick Warren, in his book, *The Purpose Driven Life*, writes:

> In the New Testament, people were baptized as soon as they believed. At Pentecost, 3,000 were baptized the same day they accepted Christ. Elsewhere, an Ethiopian leader was baptized on the spot when he was converted, and Paul and Silas baptized a Philippian jailer at midnight. There are no delayed baptisms in the New Testament. If you haven't been baptized as an expression of your faith in Christ, do so as soon as possible, as Jesus commanded.[20]

Baptism is the obedient act that publicly symbolizes that you have been separated from what you were before Christ and proclaims what you are now in Christ. Through baptism, your death, burial, and resurrection with Jesus Christ is symbolized. Baptism represents spiritual truth but does not bestow any supernatural grace or life upon the person being baptized.

Remember: It is Christ alone who provides our salvation—not Christ *plus* baptism. Have you been baptized as a believer in Jesus Christ?

Some churches baptize infants; maybe you were one of those whose parents brought you to church to be baptized. The custom of infant baptism began about 300 years after the Bible was completed. It's a ceremony intended to emphasize a commitment between the parents and God on the behalf of the child. During this ceremony, the parents promise to raise their child in the faith until the child is old enough to make his own personal confession of Christ. Therefore, if you were baptized as a baby, I strongly encourage you to be baptized again—by immersion—as a believer in Jesus Christ.

Whether a child or an adult, if you have come to Jesus Christ, you have received the Holy Spirit. Jesus Himself commands you now to follow His example and be baptized.

CHAPTER FOUR

The Lord's Supper:
A Celebration of Mankind's Deliverance

Communion. The Lord's Supper. A number of images may come to your mind when you think of this topic. Let me ask: do you ever think of grape juice?

Some churches observe Communion by drinking wine. In the church I pastor, we drink grape juice to celebrate the Lord's Supper. Here's a true and interesting story about this grape juice.

A young couple was accepted to be missionaries in Africa. On the day they were to leave, they reported to the dock in New York City from where their ship was to depart. It was here, as they were ready to board, that the wife's doctor strongly advised against them going to Africa because of her poor health; he said Africa's climate would kill her. The missionaries, especially the young man, were heartbroken but confident in God's providence. They returned to their home. The young man was then fully determined to make all the money he could to be used for sharing the gospel to the most far-reaching points on earth.

In 1869, this young missionary's father—a physician and dentist by profession—successfully pasteurized Concord grape juice to produce an unfermented sacramental wine for fellow parishioners at his church in Vineland, New Jersey, where he was a communion steward. The young man, who had followed his father in dentistry but later left that profession, took the juice-making business over, developing it until it became a vast enterprise making large amounts of money. By 1893, grape juice became a national favorite as thousands sampled it at the Chicago World's Fair. Our young man with a heart for the world, Dr. Charles E. Welch, and the company he founded, now known as Welch's, has literally given millions of dollars to the work of missions around the globe.[1]

Let's go beyond the grape juice, the bread, and the silver trays, and see what God wants to tell us about this ordinance of His Church. The apostle Paul, in writing to the Corinthian church, had this to say:

> In the following directives I have no praise for you, for your meetings do more harm than good. In the first place, I hear that when you come together as a church, there are divisions among you, and to some extent I believe it. No doubt there have to be differences among you to show which of you have God's approval. So then, when you come together, it is not the Lord's Supper you eat, for when you are eating, some of you go ahead

with your own private suppers. As a result, one person remains hungry and another gets drunk. Don't you have homes to eat and drink in? Or do you despise the church of God by humiliating those who have nothing? What shall I say to you? Shall I praise you? Certainly not in this matter!

For I received from the Lord what I also passed on to you: The Lord Jesus, on the night he was betrayed, took bread, and when he had given thanks, he broke it and said, "This is my body, which is for you; do this in remembrance of me." In the same way, after supper he took the cup, saying, "This cup is the new covenant in my blood; do this, whenever you drink it, in remembrance of me." For whenever you eat this bread and drink this cup, you proclaim the Lord's death until he comes.

So then, whoever eats the bread or drinks the cup of the Lord in an unworthy manner will be guilty of sinning against the body and blood of the Lord. Everyone ought to examine themselves before they eat of the bread and drink from the cup. For those who eat and drink without discerning the body of Christ eat and drink judgment on themselves. That is why many among you are weak and sick, and a number of you have fallen asleep. But if we were more discerning with regard to ourselves, we would not come under such judgment. Nevertheless, when we are judged in this way by the Lord, we are being disciplined so that we will not be finally condemned with the world.

So then, my brothers and sisters, when you gather to eat, you should all eat together. Anyone who is hungry should eat something at home, so that when you meet together it may not result in judgment.[2]

What we call Communion was initiated by Jesus at Passover. He transformed the Passover meal into the celebration of the infinitely greater deliverance. Passover commemorates Israel's deliverance out of Egyptian slavery; Communion communicates and celebrates mankind's deliverance from hell. When we remember His body and blood, we remember the spiritual and eternal redemption that He bought and paid for His loved ones.[3]

A Reminder of the Cross

In the book of Acts, Dr. Luke relates that the four marks of daily living for the early Christians were:

1. Obedience to the apostles' teaching
2. Fellowship
3. Breaking of bread
4. Prayer

The breaking of bread included frequent celebration of the Lord's Supper. Some scholars even believe that Communion, in some households, was celebrated at every meal.

When Pliny was governor of Bithynia, he wrote to the Roman emperor Trajan and asked as to why Christians were being systematically exterminated. He writes:

> *They asserted, however, that the sum and substance of their fault or error had been that they were accustomed to meet on a fixed day before dawn and sing responsively a hymn to Christ as to a god, and to bind themselves by oath, not to some crime, but not to commit fraud, theft, or adultery, not falsify their trust, nor to refuse to return a trust when called upon to do so. When this was over, it was their custom to depart and to assemble again to partake of food—but ordinary and innocent food. Even this, they affirmed, they had ceased to do after my edict by which, in accordance with your instructions, I had forbidden political associations. Accordingly, I judged it all the more necessary to find out what the truth was by torturing two female slaves who were called deaconesses. But I discovered nothing else but depraved, excessive superstition.*[4]

The early church developed a special fellowship meal that became known as the "love feast" that was usually closed with an observance of the Lord's Supper. It was to this that Pliny was referring. These times together emphasized oneness that led very naturally into a celebration of the unifying accomplishment of Jesus Christ on the Cross. The church at Corinth followed this custom but had turned the meals into a gluttonous, drunken revelry. When that is connected with the Lord's Supper of remembrance, it becomes a stench in God's nostrils.

In 1 Corinthians 11:17, Paul had no praise for them; he pinned their ears back! And for good reason. He used the term *"the following directives,"* which meant to command or to pass along from one to another. The phrase was used especially for an order given by a military commander and passed along the service lines by one of his subordinates. Paul is letting them know this is not his personal advice. He wants them to understand in no uncertain terms that what he's sharing with them is coming as divinely inspired instruction by and from God.

He forthrightly wrote, *". . . your meetings do more harm than good."* In other words, it would be better if you did not observe the Lord's Supper than observe it the way you are now. A time of loving fellowship and spiritual enrichment had been turned into a time of mocking the poorer members in the church, selfish indulgence, ridiculing the Lord's death, and scandalizing the church before the eyes of the world. Paul calls the Corinthians to sanctify—to make holy once again—the Lord's Supper. He discusses their perversion of it, the Lord's purpose for it, and the right preparation for it.

The Perversion of the Lord's Supper

The word "church" in the New Testament is the Greek word, *ekklesia*, which means an *assembly* or *called out ones*. The word is never used as a building or meeting place; it is always used of believers and followers of Jesus Christ. Apparently this assembly of called out ones bickered and argued whenever they met.

Paul said that he had heard of divisions among them. The word *divisions* comes from the Greek word *schismata*, from which we derive our word schism. It literally refers to cutting or tearing. They could not agree on anything, nor did they seek to serve each other. They tore their fellowship apart. Instead of sharing the love of Christ from a place of love, unity, and fellowship, they spent their time in selfish indulgence, arguing, and disputing. Paul may have been hearing these things second or thirdhand, (verse 18 "*I hear that . . .*"), so he wanted to give them the benefit of the doubt. He added, "*to some extent I believe it.*" These reports, however, were not hard for Paul to believe. Earlier in his letter, he spoke very pointedly about their divisions based on party loyalty. These divisions ended in quarrels.

The church members were also divided socially. The well-off members brought food and ate it before the poorer members could share in it. This was a far cry from the Christians in Jerusalem who, "*. . . committed themselves to the teaching of the apostles, the life together, the common meal, and the prayers.*"[5] Here in Corinth, it was every man for himself; the upper class in the Corinthian church wouldn't even share in a "potluck" supper with their less fortunate brothers and sisters.

Earlier in his letter, Paul appealed to them:

> *I appeal to you, dear brothers and sisters, by the authority of our Lord Jesus Christ, to live in harmony with each other. Let there be no divisions in the church. Rather, be of one mind, united in thought and purpose.*[6]

Paul then continued, *"Brothers and sisters, in the past I could not talk to you as I talk to spiritual people. I had to talk to you as I would to people without the Spirit—babies in Christ."*[7]

They were walking in the flesh rather than in the Spirit, following their own desires and wills—not the will of Jesus Christ. Division in a church is one of the first and surest signs of spiritual sickness. Pastor and author Dr. John MacArthur writes, *"One of the first symptoms of worldliness and backsliding, often before it shows up in compromised doctrine or life-style, is dissension within a congregation."*[8]

The Paradox

In all of this mess, we now see a rather unique paradox (and, no, a paradox is not two doctors!), the silver lining in the cloud. Here it is: it was necessary for there to be factions within the Corinthian church in order to *"show which of you has God's approval"* (1 Corinthians 11:19).

Anywhere there are people there will be differences of opinions. If you think you've found the perfect church, don't go there; you'll make it imperfect! Paul knew that divisions could not altogether be avoided. Jesus Himself taught us there will be tares among the wheat.[9] There will be disobedient people among the true believers.

Paul said, *"there have to be differences."* The language he employed has the idea of, *"it is necessary"* or *"it must be."* In the Book of Acts, when Peter and his cohorts were told by the Jerusalem's religious leaders to stop preaching the gospel, *"Peter and the apostles answered, 'It's necessary to obey God rather than men.'"*[10] The words, *"it's necessary,"* are the same words Paul used in 1 Corinthians. It is often used throughout the New Testament to represent divine necessity.

Back to our paradox: Paul said, *"which of you have God's approval . . ." Approval* means *that which has passed a test.* The term was used of precious metals tried in fire and proved to be pure. Church division, as ungodly as it is, nevertheless is used by the Lord to prove the worth of His faithful ones. In the midst of bickering, selfishness, and divisiveness, the godly ones rise to the top: the cream of the crop. Trouble within a church creates a situation in which true spiritual strength, wisdom, and leadership can be manifested.

Factions are not merely divisive; they are destructive. Initially they reveal the strong true character of the approved men and women in the church, the spiritual ones who are the leaders. But when left unchallenged, the divisive ones will undermine any Christian group and cannot be tolerated.

In another New Testament letter, Paul told Titus, *"If people are causing divisions among you, give a first and second warning. After that, have nothing more to do with them."*[11] The contentious person, by his carnality, proves his unfitness to be a part of Christian fellowship. Yes, it is necessary that factions appear, but it is not necessary that these be tolerated or allowed to lead to a divisive schism within the church. Someone once remarked, "You cannot prevent a bird from landing in your hair, but you can prevent him from building a nest there."

Participating Together

They were not really eating the Lord's Supper together, Paul says. They were selfishly indulging themselves in food and drink; the sacrificial death of Christ and the love for one another that is commanded by Christ never apparently made an appearance at their "love feasts."

The focal point of all this ungodly behavior was the Lord's Supper. *Supper* was the word normally used in reference to the evening meal. This was a genuine meal where the church congregated to eat and to observe the Lord's Supper. The abuses, however, led to the disappearance of this love feast. To protect the Lord's Supper, they had to be separated, and the supper, as we know it, ceased to exist.

When some of the believers ate before others arrived, the latter went hungry. Paul asked, in 1 Corinthians 11:22, *"Don't you have homes to eat and drink in? Or do you despise the church of God by humiliating those who have nothing?"* If you want to be selfish, do it at home! Or were they actually trying to destroy the fellowship of the saints? Were they so contemptuous of their poorer brothers and sisters in Christ that they intentionally wanted to publicly humiliate them? Paul said that they would not receive any approval from him in this!

Right Motives

Our attitudes and motives should be pure at all times, especially when we come to the Table of the Lord—the symbolic bread of His body and the cup of His blood. It is absolutely necessary to leave all sin, bitterness, wrath, anger, malice, racial and sexual prejudice, all class pride, and all feelings of inferiority behind. Of all places, of all occasions, these attitudes are most out of place at the Lord's Table. They grievously profane that holy, beautiful, and unifying ordinance of Almighty God.

The purpose of the Lord's Supper

Have you ever made the major purchase of a beautiful diamond? When I went to buy my wife Darlene's diamond engagement ring, the jeweler removed the stone from a packet and laid it out upon a piece of black velvet. In the midst of that blackness, the diamond shone even more beautifully.

1 Corinthians 11:23-26 is like that diamond on velvet. One of the most stirring passages in all of Scripture is set right in the middle of this strong rebuke of worldliness, carnality, and insensitive attitudes and behavior. Let's delve a little deeper into those verses.

Its authenticity

Again, Paul says, *"For I received from the Lord what I also passed on to you . . ."* This is a chain letter! Most scholars agree that this letter was written before any of the four Gospels. If that is so, this is the first biblical record of the institution of the Lord's Supper and includes direct quotes from Jesus Himself. These truths had come from Jesus Christ to Paul to the Corinthian church—and now to us.

"On the night He was betrayed . . ." Again, this is a diamond on black velvet. This beautiful celebration of the church was instituted on the night Jesus was turned over to the authorities—the night Judas kissed Him, the night Peter cut off a soldier's ear, the night Jesus was arrested.

Its background

The Lord's Supper was given to us by Christ during Passover. You may recall that in the Seder meal celebrated still in Jewish homes today, that four cups of wine are passed during the meal. After drinking the first cup, bitter herbs dipped in a fruit sauce are eaten and a message is given on the meaning of Passover. Then the first part of a hymn is sung. The second cup is passed, and the host breaks and passes around unleavened bread. Then the meal itself, which consists of the roasted sacrificial lamb, is consumed. The third cup, after prayer, is then passed, and the rest of the hymn is sung. The fourth cup, which celebrates the coming kingdom, is consumed immediately before leaving.

When Jesus broke the bread, He gave thanks. "Give thanks" is from the Greek word *eucharisteo*, from which we get our word eucharist, which some call Communion. It was the third cup that Jesus blessed and became the cup of Communion. "*After supper, he did the same thing with the cup . . .*"[12] "*. . . and when they had sung an hymn, they went out into the mount of Olives.*"[13]

Its all-encompassing nature

In 1 Corinthians 11:24, Christ said, "*This is my body which is for you.*" "*For you*" are two of the loveliest words in all of Scripture. I became a man *for you*; I gave the gospel *for you*; I suffered *for you*; I died *for you*; I rose from the grave *for you*.

Jesus gave a new covenant. The cup that had represented the lamb's blood smeared on the doorpost of every Jewish home now represents the blood of the Lamb of God, shed for the salvation of the world. The old deliverance was from Egypt to Canaan. This new deliverance is from Hell to Heaven—from eternal life without God to eternal life with God!

Passover was transformed into the Lord's Supper. Sharing in this, therefore, is not an option for the believer. We must have Communion on a regular basis if we are to be faithful to the Lord who bought us through the act we are called to remember. Not to take the Lord's Supper on a regular basis is disobedience and sin. *"Do this in remembrance of Me"* is a commandment.

For the Hebrew person, remembrance was something much more than bringing something to mind, like, "Remember that old song from high school days we loved to sing?" "Remember that car we used to drive?"

To truly remember is to go back in your mind and recapture as much of the reality and significance of an event or experience as you can. To remember Jesus and His sacrifice is to re-live with Him His life, agony, suffering, and death as much as humanly possible. When we partake of the Lord's Supper, we do not offer a sacrifice again; to do so would be a travesty at best or a heretical action of the worst magnitude. We remember His once-for-all sacrifice for us and rededicate our lives to His obedient service.

And we do this, *"until He comes."* We not only remember His death, but we envision His coming! The Lord's Supper keeps us looking forward to that grand and glorious day when *"we who are still alive and are left will be caught up together with them in the clouds to meet the Lord in the air. And so we will be with the Lord forever."*[14]

The preparation for the Lord's Supper

Re-read 1 Corinthians 11:27-34. Did you notice that Paul issues a warning? He tells us that if we're not careful, we can come to the Table of the Lord in an unworthy manner. This can happen in many ways. We can come to the Lord's Supper . . .

- Ritualistically, without engaging our hearts and minds
- Mechanically, going through the motions, without any emotions
- Flippantly, treating it lightly, not with the import it deserves
- Heretically, believing it imparts grace or merit that the ceremony itself, rather than the sacrifice of Christ that the ordinance represents, can save you or keep you saved
- Spitefully, with a spirit of bitterness or hatred toward a fellow believer
- Obstinately, with unconfessed sin of which we will not repent

If we come with anything other than the loftiest thoughts of God—His grace and mercy shown to us through the sacrificial atonement of the Lord Jesus Christ—or with anything less than total love for our brothers and sisters in Christ, then we come to the table in a manner unworthy of the Lord.

If I were to take the flag of your country and throw it down and trample upon it, I am not only dishonoring a piece of cloth, am I? I dishonor the country that this flag represents. To come unworthy to Communion is not to simply dishonor the ceremony, but the One Whom it represents. We become guilty of dishonoring His body and blood, which represents His love and grace toward us, which reminds us *that Christ died for us while we were still sinners.*[15]

Paul continues: "*So if anyone eats this bread and drinks from this cup of the Lord in an unworthy manner, he is guilty of sin against the body and the blood of the Lord.*"[16] This guilt brings judgment with it. Judgment has the idea of chastisement, not condemnation. In this case, the difference between the two is seen in verse 32, where it is clear that judgment refers to the discipline of the saved and condemnation refers to the condemnation of the lost. The Bible says, "*If you belong to Christ Jesus, you won't be punished.*"[17]

To avoid God's chastening judgment, we must come to the table properly discerning our hearts and responding to the holiness of the occasion. Paul then illustrates how God's judgment is used: "*That's why so many of you even now are listless and sick, and others have gone to an early grave.*"[18]

Wow! God does not eternally condemn those who misuse the Lord's Table, but His punishment may be severe—from illness to death. Sleep, as described here, as in several other New Testament references, is used metaphorically to speak of the death of believers. God actually put to death a number of believers in Corinth because they continually despised the Lord's Supper and corrupted it, just as He had put to death Ananias and Sapphira for lying to the Holy Spirit.[19]

Approaching in self-examination

There is a remedy, however, for unworthiness. Paul tells us in 1 Corinthians 11:31, "*But if we were more discerning with regard to ourselves, we would not come under such judgment.*" John, the beloved disciple, wrote, "*But if we confess our sins to him, he can be depended on to forgive us and to cleanse us from every wrong. And it is perfectly proper for God to do this for us because Christ died to wash away our sins."*[20]

If we come to the Lord's Supper with wrong motives, God will judge us—not toward condemnation, but to chastise us so that we might return wholly to Him. God sends disciplining judgment to push us back toward righteous behavior, and He has even sent death to some in the church to encourage those who remain to choose holiness rather than sin.

Paul closes this portion of his letter to the Corinthians by admonishing them to get their act together: straighten out your attitudes, discard your prejudices, selfishness, and indifference at the Table of the Lord. In other words, the Lord's Supper is not about me—it's all about Jesus!

When Leonardo DaVinci was forty-three years old, the Duke of Milan, Ludovico Sforza, commissioned DaVinci to paint the dramatic scene of Jesus' Last Supper. He spent three years on the assignment. He grouped the disciples in threes—two groups on either side of the central figure of Christ. Christ's arms are outstretched. He holds a cup, beautifully painted, in His right hand.

When the masterpiece was finished, he told the Duke, "Observe it and give me your opinion of it." "It's wonderful," Ludovico exclaimed. "The cup is so real I cannot divert my eyes from it!" Immediately and without a word, DaVinci took a brush and painted right across the sparkling cup. As he did so, he said, "Nothing shall detract from the figure of Christ!"[21]

The Table of the Lord. Nothing about it should ever detract from Him.

CHAPTER FIVE

Connecting:
How Do You Relate to the Church?

Who is Jesus Christ? Ask this question on any street corner in America and you might receive any one of the following responses:

The atheist will say there is no God; thus, there is no Son of God.

The Nation of Islam and its former leader Elijah Muhammad have said that Jesus was a prophet but not the equal of Muhammad, the founder of Islam.

Christian Scientists will say that Jesus was a mere man who demonstrated the Christ (or "divine life"). It does not matter whether or not He existed or if His blood sacrifice on the cross cleanses from sin.

The Freemason may answer, "We tell the sincere Christian that Jesus of Nazareth was but a man like us."

The Mormon will tell us that Jesus was the child of Adam and Mary—not born to the Virgin Mary, nor conceived by the Holy Spirit. Christ was a God-man, therefore, we can be just like Him.

The Church of Scientology, which counts Hollywood stars among its adherents, teaches that Christ was a man who achieved the "state of clear"—commendable, but not the highest state achievable. Jesus, they say, was certainly not God.

Today's sophisticated person may respond along with Julius Huxley, "Operationally, God is beginning to resemble not a ruler, but the last fading smile of a cosmic Cheshire cat." Huxley wrote in his book *Religion Without Revelation*,[1] "For my own part, the sense of spiritual relief that comes from rejecting the idea of God as a supernatural being is enormous."

Just who is Jesus Christ? Do you realize Jesus Himself asked this same question? He questioned the disciples about their faith in Him, and He inquired about the public's perception regarding Him:

> [Jesus] asked his disciples, "Who do people say that the Son of Man is?" "Well," they replied, "some say John the Baptist, some say Elijah, and others say Jeremiah or one of the other prophets." Then he asked them, "But who do you say I am?" Simon Peter answered, "You are the Messiah, the Son of the living God."[2]

Their responses were all very flattering. John the Baptist, Elijah, Jeremiah, or one of the Old Testament prophets is pretty heady company! In other words, *Jesus, your teachings are similar to theirs, and people are compar- ing You to one of them, or a new one of them.* All of these answers, of course, were wrong.

After asking the Twelve about the public's opinion of Him, Jesus asked His disciples who they thought He was. Speaking for the disciples, Peter spoke his now-famous words, *"You are the Christ, the Son of the living God."*[3] Peter used the phrase, "the Christ." He was saying Christ is the Messiah.

In Him are all the promises of God fulfilled. All the promises of God to His people Israel found their fruition in Christ. The Old and New Testaments make it clear: the Messiah is more than a human being. He is God.

Peter acknowledged Jesus as the Son of the living God. The disciples had come to this conclusion as they observed Jesus over a period of time, listening to His teachings, witnessing His miracles, and watching His life.

What about you? What do you say? British author C. S. Lewis in his book, *God in the Dock*, writes:

> *He went about saying to people, "I forgive your sins." Now it is quite natural for a man to forgive something you do to him. Thus if somebody cheats me out of five pounds it is quite possible and reasonable for me to say, "Well, I forgive him, we will say no more about it." What on earth would you say if somebody had done you out of five pounds and I said, "That is all right, I forgive him?"*
>
> *A man who was merely a man and said the sort of things Jesus said wouldn't be a great moral teacher. He'd either be a lunatic—on*

the level with a man who says he's a poached egg—or else he'd be the devil of hell. You must make your choice. Either this man was, and is, the Son of God, or else a madman or something worse. [4]

Peter, the other disciples, and people from all walks of life and backgrounds, have observed Him and say collectively through Peter, "You are the Christ, the Son of the living God." Millions of people from ages past to present day have likewise made their personal declaration of faith in Christ.

Once a person has made a public declaration of their belief in Jesus Christ, who He is and what He has done, the Bible teaches us that our next step is to be baptized. After baptism, unfortunately, too many new followers of Jesus think that's all there is.

After public declarations of faith in Christ and baptism, the Bible clearly teaches us that we are to belong to a local group of believers—a church. The next time you are reading in one of the four Gospels (Matthew, Mark, Luke, and John), observe that when Jesus asked someone to follow Him, if they responded with a "yes," the next step was relational: join with those people who were also following Jesus in a faith community, whose mission was to obey His teachings, and then go out and change the world!

We see this enacted in the second chapter of Acts. Peter, (yes, that same Peter), proclaimed the gospel story of Jesus in the city of Jerusalem, and more than 3,000 responded to his message. What happened next to those thousands, Dr. Luke, the author of Acts, tells us:

All the believers devoted themselves to the apostles' teaching, and to fellowship . . . and shared everything they had . . . they worshiped together . . . they shared their meals with great joy and generosity . . .[5]

This wasn't just some loosely, thrown together conglomeration of people. This teaching and fellowship and sharing and worshiping had a name: The Church of Jesus Christ.

The word *church* is an interesting one. As we saw in the previous chapter, in the Greek language of the New Testament, it's the word *ekklesia*. It means "the called-out ones" or "assembly." We are called out *from*, and we are called out *to*; we're called to be separate from the world and yet called to the world around us. We gather together with our spiritual faith family with a mission to fulfill. That mission is referred to as the Great Commission. Jesus taught us:

"All authority has been given to Me in heaven and on earth. Go therefore and make disciples of all the nations, baptizing them in the name of the Father and the Son and the Holy Spirit, teaching them to observe all that I commanded you; and lo, I am with you always, even to the end of the age."[6]

Hand-in-hand with the Great Commission we find Jesus' Great Commandment. He was once asked by a lawyer who was trying to trip Him up by his questioning, *"Teacher, which is the great commandment in the Law?"*

> *. . . [Jesus] said to him, "'You shall love the Lord your God with all your heart, and with all your soul, and with all your mind.' This is the great and foremost commandment. The second is like it, 'You shall love your neighbor as yourself.' On these two commandments depend the whole Law and the Prophets."[7]*

In those two profound statements, Jesus provides us with our God-given purposes for life and the God-given purposes for church. He says we must first connect with God. When we love Him with our heart, soul, and mind, that's what happens. Then, He commissions us to teach and disciple and baptize—that's helping people grow and mature in their faith walk. He also tells us to love our neighbor: that's service.

Then He commands us to go to all the nations, He's teaching that we are to take the gospel everywhere and to every people group (the word *nations* in Matthew 28:29 means a large group of people based on various cultural, physical, or geographical ties[8]). We are, therefore, to reach the world. All of this is to be undergirded and rooted in worship. When we love Him, we will worship Him every day and in every way.

There is purpose to your life and mine given by Jesus: connect, grow, serve, reach, and worship. We are to live out these faith components in our lives both individually and corporately.

The question for you is this: "Am I a member of a church yet?"

Being in the ministry for more than thirty-five years, I have heard all sorts of reasons and excuses for why people answer "no" to that question. Some don't like the idea of having their names on a membership roll. These are the same people whose names are on the rolls of homeowners associations, fitness clubs, country clubs, hobby clubs, the PTA, voter registration, sports leagues, fraternal organizations, unions, and, well, you get the idea.

Is the church just another organization to add to the list? Not if you begin to see it as Jesus does, He said, ". . . I [am putting] together my church, a church so expansive with energy that not even the gates of hell will be able to keep it out."[9]

Others might say that they find church in other settings. I've lost track of the number of people who have told me that their church is the outdoors (usually confined to a golf course or a boat!). Or their Bible study group is their church. Or their campus ministry is their church, or the television ministry they watch and send money to monthly is their church.

Let's be crystal clear: anything people insert in place of what the Holy Spirit birthed in Acts 2 is a counterfeit of the true church Jesus instituted. We can't just call anything a church, even if it's a gathering of Christians. Any old gathering of Christians does not constitute a church. If everything is the church, then nothing is the church.

The Bible is clear. The church is a clearly defined community, rallying around God's purposes, made up of every ethnicity, language, race, gender, and age. Let's also be clear on this point: the church is not a building. The church is people. Ask most people where they attend church, and they will reference a particular name connected to a geographical location with a physical facility. That's where the church meets, but that's not the church. (I was humorously reminded of this when my wife, Darlene, and I met some teenage girls from a church in Alabama. We were all attending the same conference and the cafeteria-style dining arrangement meant that we often sat with strangers. Seeking to make conversation, I asked the students if their church was a large church. One of the young ladies matter-of-factly told me, "It's a two-story!")

The Church of Jesus has clearly defined roles for its members, even offices for some of its leaders such as pastor, evangelist, elder, or deacon. It is a faith community that willingly submits to the authority of God's Word, the Bible, where those who preach and teach are faithfully expounding and applying God's Word to God's people.

The church gathers frequently and regularly to worship as the family of God, observing the two ordinances Jesus left for us: baptism and the Lord's Supper. The church serves God by serving those both within and outside the local faith family—all the while taking the gospel of Christ locally, regionally, nationally, and internationally.

Furthermore, in the book of Acts, and in the subsequent New Testament books, we discover two analogies: one of the invisible church and another of the visible church.

The invisible church is made up of the truly believing; only God knows who they are. They encompass the church past, present, and future. God alone is the Judge of the authenticity of our outwardly confessed faith. Whether or not you are in or out of this invisible church is known only to God.

The visible church is made up of people professing to have faith in Christ. In *The Purpose Driven Life*, author and pastor Rick Warren writes:

> *Except for a few important exceptions referring to all believers throughout history, almost every time the word church is used in the Bible, it refers to a local visible congregation. The New Testament assumes membership in a local congregation. The only Christians not members of a local fellowship were those under church discipline who had been removed from the fellowship because of gross public sin.*[10]

On a practical level, church membership is an expression of obedience to God, through submission to the elders of the church. Apart from this authority structure, leaders cannot lead, and members have no one to follow, being like sheep without a shepherd. Thus, local church membership is essential to the proper functioning of the Body of Christ.

It is not unlikely that today, as a newcomer to your relationship with the Lord Jesus, that you may hear other believers downplay the importance of local church membership. Some even go so far as to reject the notion of church membership altogether. This de-emphasis on formally uniting with a local church is part of a stance that does not fall in line with Scriptural values. We live in an age where very few want to be committed to anything: a job, a country, or even their marriage. This attitude has even produced a generation of "church shoppers and hoppers." Church membership swims against the current of America's consumer mentality. It is an unselfish decision.

Every person, therefore, who publicly identifies as a follower of Christ is to be a member of a church—card-carrying, signed-on, all-in, name-on-the-dotted-line member. As the apostle Paul wrote, "*. . . you are members of God's very own family . . . and you belong in God's household with every other Christian.*"[11]

CHAPTER SIX

Spiritual Maturity:
Growing as a Follower of Jesus

I hold a belief that the key to systematic, healthy spiritual growth in someone's life begins with their morning hours. In other words, connecting with God in the morning hours of our day can be a springboard to taking Him with us throughout the remainder of our day. (This is not always a popular opinion!)

Some reading this will agree and say, "Yes! Love those morning hours!" Others don't believe in God before 11:00 a.m. and four cups of coffee. The entire human race can often be placed in one of two camps: morning people and non-morning people. They have very little in common, and they often marry one another.

Morning people wake up with a smile, ready to tackle their to-do list. They are excited to greet the day, and they head into it ready to go. The flip side is that at about 9:00 p.m., they're slipping into Neverland.

I have a few close friends who literally begin their days between 3:30 and 4:00 a.m. (That's not a typo; you read that correctly. Personally, I think that if you wake up that early, you'd better be getting up to milk cows!) Maybe mornings are not your thing. You don't sleep in until noon; you still have to awaken early for work or school, but you're not a fan. You don't like it. Morning people are like "Heigh-ho! Heigh-ho! It's off to work I go!" And non-morning people are cussing. That's the big difference.

If you're a non-morning person, how many times over the years have you felt guilty that you're not a morning person? My guess is more often than not. You may feel that way because we constantly read or hear that the most productive people in society are the ones who are up early and accomplish more before 8:00 a.m. than most people do all day. And that makes us feel guilty. Sure, we can get stuff done at night, but it's not the same.

Or is it?

I think it's interesting that as you look at the life of Jesus, you find that He was just as much a night owl as a morning person. I don't think we always see that. Maybe you grew up in church and often heard the Bible verse, *"In the early morning, while it was still dark, Jesus got up, left the house, and went away to a secluded place, and was praying there."*[1]

Jesus was a morning person. What we often don't realize, however, is that He also prayed and went to be alone at night; He was a night person, too. I find that Jesus went to be by Himself to have some alone time with God in the evening just as much as He did in the morning. Jesus didn't seem to favor one time over the other. I don't think

Jesus was a morning person or a non-morning person; I think Jesus was more of a God-person.

Consider the following action steps that you can take daily to awaken intimacy with God and recognize His presence in your life. When that happens, spiritual growth occurs. Spiritual growth is not a program, or a system, or a plan, as much as it is simply spending time alone with God.

These steps will help you hold the hand of God so that as you go through your day, you are not walking alone. There is something to beginning our day off right, so consider what we can do in the morning to set our day's trajectory for spiritual growth and maturity.

Action Step 1—Praise Him!

In the initial moments immediately upon waking up, take a few moments to turn your heart to the worship of God and rejoice in who He is. Moses wrote, *"Acknowledge and take to heart this day that the Lord is God in heaven above and on the earth below. There is no other."*[2]

The Bible says to acknowledge that this day. The acknowledgement of your allegiance to Him is a great way to begin your day. Think this through with me: we ought to begin our day by lying in bed! This concept may be delectable to you, and you're thinking, "I can do that! I like this approach already." This is not, however, about grabbing some additional shuteye; this is the discipline of being still for a few moments, which can be a challenge for both morning and non-morning people.

For many morning people, the last thing they want to do is be still. Many wake up, leap out of bed, and head right into the day. If that describes you, why not try to be still for a moment tomorrow morning and begin the day with words that acknowledge God? You can use words that confess His greatness and His ownership, words that acknowledge your dependence on His role in your life—all before your feet ever touch the floor.

If you will condition yourself so that even before you get out of bed you go to the Lord with praise and thanksgiving for who He is, it will better your life. This is not about prayer as we often think of it. This is about worship: simply acknowledging who God is and that the day belongs to Him.

If you're a non-morning person, this may be more of a challenge for you. One of the last things a non-morning person wants to do is talk to anyone early in the day. Most non-morning people are not verbal in the morning, and so their thoughts don't usually lean toward talking to God. They won't talk to anybody, and if they are forced to, they will sound like Chewbacca from Star Wars.

Why is it a good idea to begin our day with words of worship? Words of worship immediately place you in the mode of recognizing God's presence in your life. You start your day by thinking, "God, I want to recognize who You are because as soon as I step out of bed, I want to be on track with You."

This one step alone will help you to become a better person, a better parent, a better spouse, a better child, a better employee, a better Christ-follower. If you want to get practical here, you may need to write down some words of worship on an index card and keep that by the bed. (I recommend that instead of using a notes app on your phone. Tablets and cell phones can become a distraction in a nanosecond.) Begin by taking your blank card and thumb through the Book of Psalms. Jot down a dozen terms or so and keep them by the side of your bed; words like awesome, worthy, blessed, shield, rock or fortress. When you need to prime the spiritual pump in the morning, read those words of worship back to God. You could begin that tomorrow (or after a nap today!).

I guarantee if you do this, it will begin to change the way you think about your day, yourself, your faith, about God, and about the world. You'll find yourself rejoicing in the Lord, and you won't even be out of bed yet!

The second thing I'd encourage you to do is to reflect.

Action Step 2—Recall What He Has Done For You

The Psalmist wrote, *"May the Lord be praised, for he has wonderfully shown his faithful love to me..."*[3] We need a daily reminder of God's love. Some people don't think they need to be reminded of God's love every day; I would question that. I think you do. I need to be reminded that God is crazy about me, that He loves me no matter what, and that I'm not just a number on this planet. I need that because I will face people in my day who are going to have negative feelings about me.

Can I let you in on a little secret? Not everyone likes you; not everybody likes me either. As difficult as it for you and me to believe, there are people in the world, in the marketplace, in neighborhoods, in sports, at school, wherever we go, that don't like us. They'd love to see us fail. Welcome to a sinful and fallen world, otherwise known as reality!

One of the great ways to defend yourself against that certainty is to be reminded of your worth in God's eyes. Perhaps you do that while still in bed or perhaps as you go about your process of getting ready in the morning. You can also do that as you get in the shower in the morning. As the water jets out of the showerhead, you can allow the water to remind you of God's love showering down on you. We all need morning-hour reminders:

- That reminder that God loves you.
- That reminder that you are created in the image of God.
- That reminder that you are fearfully and wonderfully made.
- That reminder that the author of the universe loves you so much that He sent His Son Jesus to die on the cross in your place.

Within minutes, therefore, of being awake you can rejoice with words of worship and you can reflect on your value and worth to God.

The third thing I'd like to encourage you to do is to read.

Action Step 3—Open God's Word

The Psalmist wrote, "*I have hidden Your word in my heart, that I might not sin against You,*"[4] and, "*Your word is a lamp to guide my feet and a light for my path.*"[5]

This is the action step where you take some time with the Bible, and you hide God's Word in your heart. Hide it there so that God's Word will guide you and speak to you, so that you can recall it throughout the day. It will guide the way that you live in a dark world.

Everybody understands the value of reading but not everyone does it. Why not? Whenever I talk to people about why they don't read the Bible, they usually come up with one of three reasons.

The first reason sounds exactly like this: "I don't have the time." That's really not a reason; it's an excuse. And a fairly lame excuse at that. Here's why: we always make time for what we value and what we think is important. Always.

The second most popular reason that I hear is that they didn't understand the Bible when they read it in the past. That reason is more plausible. There are sections of the Bible that are difficult to understand. There are, however, things we can do to help that, such as reading Scripture in a more understandable, easier-to-read translation. There are dozens of translations available in everyday English (to find out more about Bible translations and helpful Bible study resources, please see the Addendum in the back of this book).

I always encourage people to read from a translation rather than a paraphrase. There is a difference between the two. Our friends at gotquestions.org provide some very helpful guidance on this:

> A paraphrase is a retelling of something in your own words. A paraphrase of the Bible is different from a translation in that a translation attempts (to varying degrees) to communicate as "word-for-word" or as "thought-for-thought" as possible. A paraphrase takes the meaning of a verse or passage of Scripture and attempts to express the meaning in "plain language"—essentially the words the author of the paraphrase would use to say the same thing. The most popular example of a Bible paraphrase would be "The Message" by Eugene Peterson.

Many people use paraphrases as their "reading Bible," preferring to read straight through as with a novel. This can be particularly helpful in long narrative passages such as found in Genesis, 1 and 2 Kings, and 1 and 2 Chronicles. Then they use actual translations—such as the New American Standard, New King James, and New International Version—for in-depth reading and study.

Should you use a paraphrase? A paraphrase of the Bible should not be used as a Christian's primary Bible. We have to remember that a paraphrase is what the author thinks the Bible says, not necessarily what the Bible says.[6]

The third reason I often hear people give is: "I don't know where to start." What often happens is that people take the Bible and read it like a regular book, starting at the beginning, progressing from cover to cover. This makes total sense. All your life you've been taught to read a book at the beginning, moving toward the end.

The Bible, though, isn't just any book. Many people assume that when they start, they should read Genesis and then Exodus. It usually starts off well doing it this way. Genesis and Exodus both contain moving accounts revolving around seismic encounters with God and people whose names we may well be familiar with already.

Then they hit the book of Leviticus, and suddenly they're reading about the eighth animal sacrifice on the fourth hill with the twelfth priest's blessing, and, well, you know what happens: "Have I checked Instagram lately?" If they survive Leviticus, they get to the Book of

Numbers, which is just what it sounds like (many lists and numbers and names). Suppose they power through Numbers and make it to Deuteronomy. Do you know what Deuteronomy means? It means "Second Law" or "the Law a Second Time." Deuteronomy contains a number of things they read already in Leviticus, most of it making no sense at all to them. It's no wonder why some people give up and quit Bible reading!

If you are just getting started reading the Bible, I encourage you to begin in a wonderful book of the New Testament: The Gospel of John. Start there and read to the end of the New Testament. Beginning with John means that you will begin your Bible reading with the life of Jesus, and then you'll get the history of the church in the book of Acts and some practical faith teaching in the book of Romans.

Another piece of advice is to be practical. Sometimes we'll say, "I'm going to read through the Bible in a year." We find an online reading list and join in a Bible-reading marathon group that about 0.01 percent of people ever complete.

The ultimate result of that approach succeeds quite often in making you feel guilty. To read through the Bible in a year, you have to read three or four chapters a day, without missing a day, and for a while you'll do fine.

Let's assume you start at the beginning of the year. "It's my New Year's resolution," you tell yourself. You're crushing it from January 1-10. By the time July rolls around, however, you're 287 chapters behind, which includes skipping Leviticus altogether. And then you skip Ezekiel. You never even get a whiff of the New Testament.

Let me give you a little hope. There is no place in the Bible (that I can find) that tells us how often we should read it or how quickly to complete it. As I've heard it said, "The encouragement of the Bible is that we read it for depth and not for distance."

Jesus invited us to come to Him, telling us that His burden is easy, and His yoke is light.[7] He wants us to take pleasure in Him and enjoy time with Him and time with His Word—not to feel burdened down by it.

Should you read the Bible? Absolutely. Daily? I can make a strong case for that. You may not be, however, in the habit of any Bible reading at all. Now that you know where to start (John's Gospel), just how do you start? What if you started with two minutes today and tomorrow and the next day and so on? What if you decided, "For two minutes a day, I'm going to read to develop an appetite"? Those two minutes may quickly turn into five or ten minutes.

It was Aristotle who voiced a strong and powerful statement. He said, "Living a virtuous life is a series of habitual choices." Likewise, growing and maturing as a Christ-follower is a series of tiny choices that you and I make every day that shape the type of Christian we are and that we become. My prayer for you is that you will grow to love God's Word. He's gifted us with a wonderful promise in His Word: *"Those who love Your teachings will find true peace, and nothing will defeat them."*[8] Lastly, I encourage you to take the fourth step.

Action Step 4—Talk to Him

Take a few moments in the day's initial hours to reveal your thoughts, hurts, cares, and plans to God in prayer.

Similar to Bible reading, please don't get hung up on the amount of time you need to pray. But I do want to encourage you to take some time during your morning to focus on a connection with God.

You will read more about prayer in chapter nine, but perhaps a few words from a different perspective here will prove helpful. When you pray in the morning, you are simply jump-starting a conversation that will continue throughout your day. That was eye-opening to me when I realized that. I wasn't just getting one more thing done and crossing it off my list. I was beginning a conversation that would carry on throughout the day. Perhaps as you drive to work or school imagine Jesus in the seat next to you and talk to Him. As you move throughout your day, share with Him about how things are going. Share your joys and your burdens with Him. The conversation you carry on with Him throughout your day starts in the morning hours.

In his book *Too Busy Not to Pray,* Bill Hybels says:

> *It boils down to this. If you are willing to invite God to involve Himself in your daily life, you will experience His prevailing power. That power may come in the form of wisdom, an idea that you desperately need and can't come up with yourself. It may come in the form of courage, greater than you could ever muster. It may come in the form of confidence or perseverance, uncommon staying power, changed attitude toward a spouse or child or a parent. Or a changed circumstance. Maybe even outright miracles. However it comes, God's prevailing power is released in the lives of people who pray.*[9]

Let's end this chapter with a challenge by answering the question, "Now what?" Answer: Get started. Get started with any of these action steps. Pick one. Develop that habit and begin to add the others. Or jump in tomorrow morning with all four—whatever fits you best right now at this season in your life.

Here's why it's so important. I meet so many wonderful people who are in desperate need of a meaningful, powerful relationship with God, but they're not experiencing it. They may even carry the "Christian" title. Yet they live their lives distant and unconnected from God on a daily basis. They just sort of check in with Him every once in a while.

If you want to grow spiritually mature as a follower of Jesus, then you need to arrive at the point where, even if it's just for a few minutes, you check in and connect with God. In doing so, you begin the day with Him and carry that relationship with Him throughout your entire day.

May you, even as you read these few lines, sense the gentle tug of God's Spirit upon your heart—that still, small, whispered voice that says, *"He's talking to you. This is what you need. This is for you."* Maybe a year from now, six months from now, or five years from now you'll look back on this day as the day when you awakened to the power of what it looks like to connect with God on a daily basis so that you, as the apostle Peter said, *"Grow in the grace and knowledge of our Lord and Savior Jesus Christ."*[10]

CHAPTER SEVEN

Giving:

The Sermon on the Amount

In Charles Dickens' classic *Oliver Twist*[1], the young Oliver proceeds through the orphanage dining room, holding his empty bowl in front of him. Walking directly over to stand before the stern orphanage director, he asks, "Please, sir, I want some more." The irritated director exclaims, "What?!" and hits Oliver over the head with a ladle. Oliver was ordered into instant confinement, and the next morning, a notice was posted on the outside gate, offering a reward to anyone who would take Oliver Twist off their hands.

Everything would have been fine for poor Oliver Twist if he'd simply been content with what he had. All he wanted was a bit more porridge, and instead he found himself in a heap of trouble and a lump on his head! Oliver is a symbol of our lives, you know. Desiring more typically causes problems, from the need to have more possessions to the financial pressures brought on by overused credit cards—all due to our addictive nature to accumulate and acquire.

Money can be a great blessing, but the key to it is what you think of it. Sometimes we hear people say, "If I had a million dollars, I'd give a lot to the Lord!" No, they wouldn't. The question is not what you or I would do with a million; the question is, "What am I doing with the twenty dollars in my pocket?"

The Cautions of Loving Money

Solomon, the wisest man besides Jesus Christ who ever lived, tells us:

> Whoever loves money never has money enough; whoever loves wealth is never satisfied with his income . . . As goods increase so do those who consume them. And what benefit are they to the owners except to feast their eyes on them?"[2]

The Living Bible puts it this way, "So what is the advantage of wealth—except perhaps to watch it as it runs through your fingers!"[3]

It is not a question of having more and doing more with it. It is a question of what we do with what we presently have. "Jesus told his disciples, 'Do you have any idea how difficult it is for the rich to enter God's kingdom?'"[4] Rich people often have more problems, solely because of money.

The apostle Paul wrote to young Timothy, saying, *"For the love of money is at the root of all kinds of evil. And some people, craving money, have wandered from the faith and pierced themselves with many sorrows."*[5] Notice he does not say that money is the root of all evil. It says the *love* of money is the root of all evil. We can have a lot of it and not love it, or we can have very little but love what we have. It's the love of money, not money itself. It's a question of attitude. What is your attitude toward one of the most powerful forces in life?

What ingredients make up your normal week? Time, talent, and energy are our life in our normal week. At week's end, all of these three are put into a paycheck. That is life energy symbolized by a paycheck. That's why God considers our paychecks so important.

Paul also said to Timothy:

> *A devout life does bring wealth, but it's the rich simplicity of being yourself before God. Since we entered the world penniless and will leave it penniless, if we have bread on the table and shoes on our feet, that's enough. But if it's only money these leaders are after, they'll self-destruct in no time. Lust for money brings trouble and nothing but trouble. Going down that path, some lose their footing in the faith completely and live to regret it bitterly ever after.*[6]

Godliness and contentment go together. The Bible says, *". . . be content with such things as you have."*[7] If a person loves money, you'll find that person's life rife with problems. For those who love money, but do not have much, there will be judgmental attitudes, jealousy, covetousness, and other inward contaminants. Those loving money, and also having plenty of it, will struggle with possessiveness and the temptation to hoard it for themselves or lord it over others.

Paul referred to *"People who want to get rich . . ."*[8] That is tantamount to loving money. People say, "I'm going to make a million and give it to the Lord." Don't make a million for the Lord; He doesn't need it! The Psalmist says that He already owns *"the cattle upon a thousand hills."*[9] Your little molehill doesn't mean anything to the Creator of the universe who owns it all anyway! (It's interesting to note here that the word for *money* is the Greek word, *philarguria* from *phileo*, to love, and *arguros*, silver.)

Don't cloak your desire to accumulate wealth in a spiritual dress. Seek first His kingdom, and His righteousness, and then let God worry about whether or not to give you a million dollars.

The apostle also mentioned, *". . . destruction and ruin . . ."*[10] Destruction can also literally mean "loss." When a person loves money, he is lost to God; therefore, he is useless to God. Jesus said, *"You cannot serve two masters: God and money. For you will hate one and love the other, or else the other way around."*[11] Money is also translated mammon, an Aramaic word commonly meaning riches. It is very similar to a Hebrew word which means to be firm or steadfast, hence, that which is to be trusted. Money was trusted instead of God many times throughout the Bible.

For money, Achan brought defeat on Israel's army and death to himself and his family.

For money, Ananias and Sapphira became the first hypocrites in the church, and their lives were extinguished as a testimony against the misuse of money and their deceit.

For money, Delilah betrayed Samson.

For money, Judas sold Jesus.

These folks are not very good examples for money-lovers.

The Consequences of Loving Money

Since God warns us against loving money, we should understand what loving money can do to us.

Loving money can lead you to forget about God.

Most of the book of Proverbs, with the exception of the thirtieth chapter, was written by Solomon. Proverbs 30 was penned by a man named Agur. He wrote,

> Banish lies from my lips and liars from my presence. Give me enough food to live on, neither too much nor too little. If I'm too full, I might get independent, saying, "God? Who needs him?"[12]

Loving money can cause you to forget God.

Loving money can cause you to stop trusting God.

When you have a lot of money, you begin to trust in it: "My bank account is built up."

"I've got no real worries now. If something does happen, I'm all right."

"We've got enough set aside for our retirement. We won't have any real worries then."

This may all be well and good, but if that attitude is planted, watered, and fertilized, we stop trusting God and begin trusting in riches. The Bible says, *"If I have put my trust in money, if my happiness depends on wealth . . . it would mean that I denied the God of heaven."*[13] If we depend on our money, then we deny God. Solomon writes, *Trust in your money and down you go! Trust in God and flourish as a tree!*[14] Again, Paul writes to Timothy:

> *Instruct those who are rich in this present world not to be conceited or to fix their hope on the uncertainty of riches, but on God, who richly supplies us with all things to enjoy. Instruct them to do good, to be rich in good works, to be generous and ready to share.*[15]

Do you know that the more money we get, the less we are willing to part with it? Those who know the depths of God in these matters, however, live a life countercultural to most of us. The Englishman, C. T. Studd, was a Christian and a world-class cricket player in the 1800s. When his father died, he inherited 29,000 pounds, an enormous amount of money in those days. But not wanting, as he said, "to clutter up my life," he decided to invest his money in God's work.

He gave 5,000 pounds to Hudson Taylor, who organized the China Inland Mission; 5,000 pounds to General William Booth of The Salvation Army; and 5,000 pounds to D. L. Moody to start a mission work in India. Although Moody did not go to India, the money was used, with Studd's permission, to start Moody Bible Institute in Chicago.

After all this, Studd had 3,400 pounds left, which he gave to his wife on their wedding day. Her response? "The rich ruler was asked to give all." So, they sent the remaining money to General Booth—anonymously.[16]

God's dividends started coming in, and they are still coming in today. Moody Bible Institute alone has sent out more than 47,000 missionaries around the globe.[17] All because C. T. Studd was willing to trust God when it came to money.

Loving money can cause you to be deceived.

Satan really wants to use the device of deceit against us. God wants glory out of your money, and Satan wants you to misuse it. The Bible says, "*. . . but the worries of this life, the deceitfulness of wealth, and the desires of other things come in and choke the word, making it unfruitful.*"[18] When we think we have money, we think we have everything.

The love of money can bring you to compromise biblical instruction.

Do you have a price? It is said that everybody has a price. What will you sell out for? A new car? A promotion? A new position in the company? A new house? Popularity? If you have muted the testimony of Christ in your life, because of any of these things, you have sold out. Friend, if you have a price, Satan is going to get there and make you an offer you will not believe. So be ready. Christians should not have a price because we have already been bought with the precious blood of Jesus Christ. Jesus exhorted us, "*But seek first his kingdom and his righteousness, and all these things will be given to you as well.*"[19]

Loving money can cause you to rest on unstable foundations.

Proverbs 23:4-5 says, *"Do not wear yourself out to get rich; do not trust your own cleverness. Cast but a glance at riches, and they are gone, for they will surely sprout wings and fly off to the sky like an eagle."*[20]

The love of money can cause you to be ungrateful.

Deuteronomy 8 speaks of God's provision for Israel. God warns them to beware when they are rich lest they *"forget the Lord your God . . ."*[21]

The love of money can lead to pride.

Proverbs 28:11 tells us, *"A rich man is wise in his own eyes . . ."*[22] Jeremiah 12:2 warns, *"You have planted them and they have taken root; they grow and bear fruit. You are always on their lips but far from their hearts."*[23] In other words, they were saying, "Thank you, God, for what You have given," but God wasn't really in their thoughts at all.

Loving money can also cause you to commit robbery!

It is quite possible that you might rob God. The prophet Malachi records, *"Will a man rob God? Yet you are robbing Me! But you say, 'How have we robbed You?' In tithes and offerings."*[24] You may say, "I would never rob God. I'd never steal anything from Him!" But if you keep back what you should be giving Him, then you've robbed God.

We might also be found guilty of robbing others. John, writing under the inspiration of the Holy Spirit, tells us,

"If anyone has material possessions and sees his brother or sister in need but has no pity on them, how can the love of God be in that person?"[25] The result then is that we rob our brothers and sisters in Christ.

So, you see, the whole money issue is an issue of attitude, and the wrong attitude is to love money. The proper biblical attitude is this: all money is God's, and since I am a steward of it, I should glorify God with all that He has given me. How then do we accomplish that?

The Way to Understand Money

One of the greatest principles we can ever learn in our Christian walk is this truth: God owns it all. Most every Christian will agree with this statement. We see this over and over again as God's sovereignty is revealed time and again in the Bible. There are several implications to this truth.

God can take whatever He wants, whenever He wants.

Anytime a possession is lost or a material thing is taken, you should not complain; it wasn't yours to begin with. Picture all of God's possessions entrusted to you placed in your open hand. As long as that hand remains open, God can place additional possessions there whenever He wants. When your hand begins to close, exercising control and ownership over God's possessions, God is no longer free to entrust you with more.

Every spending decision is a spiritual decision.

Once you understand God owns it all, there is nothing more or less spiritual about giving a tithe or offering than about spending money on a vacation or buying a car. In fact, if it's all God's to begin with, when you spend or give, you are saying that this is what God wants done with His resources. See how freeing this is? You can use God's resources for the accomplishment of the goals and desires that He places in your heart, with no feelings of guilt. This requires, however, regularly listening to God through His Word to determine what He wants accomplished.

Stewardship cannot be faked.

Prayer, Bible study, church attendance, witnessing and fellowship can all be faked. You can pull it off, and most people will never be the wiser. But stewardship is revealed in your checkbook. Your checkbook reveals the use of God's resources in black and white.

Ron Blue, a well-known Christian financial counselor, often asks people to take out their checkbook and picture their life story being written from that checkbook, as it reveals much about the owner of the checkbook. What sort of life story would someone write about you if all they had to go on was your checkbook?

If you recognize and acknowledge that God owns it all, how are you to give?

Giving should be in response to need.

Luke relates in Acts 4:35: *"From time to time those who owned lands and houses sold them, brought the money from the sales, and put it at the apostles' feet, and it was distributed . . ."*[26]

The early church was designed to function so that the money of the believers was brought into the church. The church leadership then invested it in eternal purposes, and they met needs. Now that doesn't mean that we are not to meet another person's needs without the church, but the dominant practice in the early church was to bring money to the church, and it would be distributed.

Further in this same book, Luke writes,

> *During this time some prophets came down from Jerusalem to Antioch. One of them, named Agabus, stood up and through the Spirit predicted that a severe famine would spread over the entire Roman world. (This happened during the reign of Claudius.) The disciples, as each one was able, decided to provide help for the brothers living in Judea.*[27]

The disciples were sensitive to a need. They heard about a need, they had a margin, and they said, "We'll all give according to our ability." From time to time, we hear of needs—a missionary, a brother or sister in the church, or a neighbor—and we should go and supply their needs. Giving should be in response to need.

Giving should be in response to God's command.

Paul shares, "*Each of you should give what you have decided in your heart to give . . .*"[28] In other words, between you and God, you need to determine what you are to give. You say, "How do I do it?" The Bible says, "*On the first day of every week, each one of you should set aside a sum of money in keeping with your income . . .*"[29] In other words, bring it and give to the Lord, through your local church, and it will be invested for eternity.

Giving should be sacrificial.

People often ask me, "How much should I give?" I
don't know, because that is between you and God, but we
can turn to Scripture for a hint. Zaccheus, when he committed his life to be a follower of Jesus, gave 50 percent for
starters. That may not be the norm, but it sure beats down
the 10 percent theory! (If you check the Old Testament
carefully, tithing is at least 23 percent a year—and up! We
do know this: tithing 10 percent is biblical and should be
a starting place for us.)

Some people may object to a teaching on tithing in a
discussion of Christian giving. "We're under grace, not
law," they say. "Christ never mentioned tithing in His
teachings." What they fail to realize is that in the era of
grace, Christians face a much higher level of expectation
from God. In comparing the demands of the law to what
He expects, in Matthew 5, Jesus said repeatedly, *"You
have heard . . . but I tell you . . ."* And His standards are
invariably higher.

When it comes to giving, grace does not settle for just
the tithe. It goes far beyond that. All we are and everything we have belongs to God. That's why the apostle Paul
commended the Macedonian believers, whose *"overflow-
ing joy and their extreme poverty welled up in rich generosity."*[30] That's why he urges all believers to *"excel in this
grace of giving."*[31]

Let's think about that for a moment. What does ex-
celled giving look like? I think we begin to discover answers when we find ourselves being known for extravagant generosity, rather than consumption or accumu-
lation. Giving that excels teaches our young to organize
their lives around giving before they get caught up in the

constant pursuit of more. When we excel in the grace of giving, people will come to know Jesus because the generosity of Christ-followers is so compelling that they will want to know the God who inspires it.

Imagine shaping your life, your world, and your culture with the value of generous giving. The freedom that giving brings transforms us into a place where we find greater joy, freedom, and purpose. We intentionally swap the temporal things of earth for treasures laid up in heaven. As a result, massive resources can be released for God's kingdom—sharing the gospel, serving the needy, and healing the world.

Giving should be secret and humble.

The Pharisees loved to let others know how much they were giving, but Jesus said do not let others know what you are giving. If you give for the sake of being seen or to have your name memorialized on a building, you have your reward. Jesus even said, "*. . . do not let your left hand know what your right hand is doing . . .*"[32] That is how secret it ought to be.

Giving is the key to spiritual fruit.

If you and I are faithful in a little, we will be faithful in much. Luke 16:10-11 says:

> *"Whoever can be trusted with very little can also be trusted with much, and whoever is dishonest with very little will also be dishonest with much. So if you have not been trustworthy in handling worldly wealth, who will you trust with true riches?"*[33]

Jesus is teaching us that if you don't handle ten dollars well, you won't handle one million dollars well. If you and I cannot handle money properly, we won't be able to handle that which is really valuable.

Jesus calls us to extravagant generosity. Rather than following Oliver Twist's example—who held out his bowl always asking for more—Christ-followers are to hold out their hands in order to extend gifts to others. Gifts that will count for eternity.

As giving believers, let's pray that God will bless and multiply what we give and will transform our lives, not by acquiring more, but by producing immeasurable gain for His eternal kingdom.

God help us to be faithful, generous stewards.

CHAPTER EIGHT

Quiet Time:
Being Alone with God

In the Christian world in which I was raised, a "quiet time" was a set-aside time of Bible reading and prayer every day, preferably in the morning; it is a wonderful way to begin the day. When I entered the Christian college I eventually graduated from, however, the quiet time was taken to a new level for me. The college was serious about its self-adopted mandate to train missionaries and ministers. They believed that to be effective in full-time ministry work, one should be disciplined—very disciplined.

Therefore, Monday through Friday of every week was regimented. Our morning began when a bell sounded at 6:15 a.m. Time to wake up. Another bell rang at 6:20. We had until that bell to sit up and get our feet on the tile floor. Sometimes hall monitors would check your promptness: if you were still horizontal through those two bells, you were written up and received a demerit (accumulate enough of those and you would find yourself cleaning something you really didn't want to clean).

We were generously gifted time from 6:20 to 6:40 to shower, shave (facial hair was frowned upon), and get dressed (try that sometime with only two shared bathrooms on a hall housing 20-25 college students!). At 6:40, another bell rang, indicating "quiet on the hall" because it was "quiet time." So, from 6:40 until 7:10 when, you guessed it, another bell rang, you were to have your morning prayer and Bible time with God—seated at your desk, not in your bed. At 7:10, we shuffled over to the cafeteria and then on to our 8:00 class.

It was legalism, pure and simple. Do this religious thing, the way we say to do it, and place yourself in the arena of God's blessing. If you didn't do it their way, then there was a penalty to be paid, (which resulted in free work for the college). The message that our young and impressionable minds received was, "You need to try harder. You need to pray more. You need to read your Bible. And you need to do it, at least, during the time we have set out for you. You need to obey the letter of the law, more than the spirit thereof." It was what one seminary professor called *sola bootstrapsa*: self-reliance. We pull ourselves up by our own spiritual bootstraps. Those who taught us such things surely meant well. The problem was not a lack of sincerity on their part. The diagnosis is far more severe. The problem was we were being sucked into a legalistic way of "doing" Christianity.

This is an indictment of people like me who preach and teach God's Word. When we lead people to believe that living the Christian life can be accomplished in our own strength and effort, we are propagating a heresy. Bryan Chapell, in his book, *Christ-Centered Preaching*, writes:

> [A]ctuating or accessing divine blessing through human works carries the message, "It is in the doing of these things that will get you right with God and/or your neighbor." No message is more damaging to true Christian faith. By making human efforts alone the measure and the cause of godliness, [we] fall victim to the twin assaults of theological liberalism and legalism— which despite their perceived opposition are actually identical in making one's relationship with God dependent upon human goodness . . . sola bootstrapsa messages are wrong, and faithful preachers must not only avoid this error but also war against it.[1]

It was decades before I was able to lay down the legalistic approach of time with God. That experience made me not even want to have a time with God. When it is regimented with clanging bells and demerits, it really takes the joy out of it. I learned that prayer is a work that must be performed. As heresies go, this one is subtle. Prayer became a duty rather than a grace. The result was a loss of joy and heaps of guilt.

This has occurred in the lives of too many Christ-followers. And prayer is not the only grace we've turned into a work. Personal Bible study has become a source of bondage as well. A whole generation of Christians have been told that God will bless them if they read their Bibles every day, as if the act of reading the Scriptures were some kind of magic talisman by which we gain power over God and secure His favor. This is not the religion of the Bible. The pervasive belief that God gives us grace as a reward for our devotional consistency is antithetical to the teachings of Jesus Christ. Prayer and Bible study—what evangelicals for the past century have called "quiet time"—have become dreaded precisely because they have been radically misunderstood.

Quiet Time Guilt

There is a ravaging disease in our churches today. It's known as QTG: Quiet Time Guilt. It's ironic, but the personal quiet time has become, I believe, the number one cause of defeat among Bible-believing Christians. At one time or another, nearly every sincere believer feels a deep sense of failure and the accompanying feelings of guilt and shame because he or she has failed to set aside a separate time for Bible study and prayer. Quiet Time Guilt is a condition with many repercussions.

The shame of Quiet Time Guilt manifests itself in an even deeper inability to fruitfully and joyfully study Scripture. Prayer becomes a dread; Bible study a burden. The Christian suffering from Quiet Time Guilt then despairs of seeing God work in his or her life, until finally he or she simply gives up. We may bravely continue outwardly with public Christian commitments like church attendance, but secretly we feel hypocritical.

What is the Cause of QTG?

The root cause of Quiet Time Guilt is legalism. Often when we think of legalism, we think of the petty man-made rules that have so often strangled the churches—rules against dancing or drinking or certain Bible translations or non-Christian music. But these legalistic rules are merely an outward sign of a deeper legalism of the heart.

When prayer and Bible study are thought of primarily as duties ("disciplines") rather than as grace, both prayer and the study of Scripture become unfruitful in our lives. We put ourselves on a performance treadmill and cease relying on God's grace to sustain us. We trust in ourselves and our consistency, becoming proud if devotionally successful—or despairing because of our devotional inconsistency. Either way, our spiritual self-reliance short-circuits the inexpressible joy of life in Christ. Quiet time becomes a human work whereby we think we gain—or lose—God's daily favor.

When we've started our day with Scripture, we presume that God's blessing will rest upon us because of it. When we fail in our quest for quiet time consistency, we feel we've short-circuited God's grace in our lives.

If you are reading this as a new follower of Jesus, there is good news! Hopefully, you haven't fallen prey to any of this yet. And now that you know about it, let's make it our goal together to avoid it. To do so, we must first recognize it, but let me tell you, the situation is far worse than you think. Even Bible study and prayer can lead us away from God if our hearts are not in the right place. Wait, did I really just say that?! I did, and here is why.

Jesus condemned the Pharisees for this very attitude about Bible study. He said, *"You study the Scriptures diligently because you think that in them you have eternal life. These are the very Scriptures that testify about me."*[2]

The Pharisees approached the Bible as a book of rules and precepts for life but failed to grasp it as a story about God's love for His people. A quiet time can drive you far from God if you fail to understand that the Scriptures are a story about His love and grace—a story about Jesus Christ, the man of grace. His works—not our works— are the center of the biblical narrative. They teach us that Jesus gives grace daily even to those who fail Him. How you and I approach the Bible—as needy sinners or as self-reliant legalists—says a lot about the state of our souls.

Just like Bible study, prayer too, can lead us away from God. Remember what Jesus said about the Pharisee and the tax collector? To some who were confident of their own righteousness and looked down on everybody else, Dr. Luke relates:

> *Then Jesus told this story to some who had great confidence in their own righteousness and scorned everyone else: "Two men went to the Temple to pray. One was a Pharisee, and the other was a despised tax collector. The Pharisee stood by himself and prayed this prayer: 'I thank you, God, that I am not like other people—cheaters, sinners, adulterers. I'm certainly not like that tax collector! I fast twice a week, and I give you a tenth of my income.'*

> *"But the tax collector stood at a distance and dared not even lift his eyes to heaven as he prayed. Instead, he beat his chest in sorrow, saying, 'O God, be merciful to me, for I am a sinner.' I tell you, this sinner, not the Pharisee, returned home justified before God. For those who exalt themselves will be humbled, and those who humble themselves will be exalted."*[3]

The religious leader saw prayer as a work, the tax collector as an expression of need. The one who merely expressed his neediness to God—the expression of our neediness being the heart of true prayer—went home right with God.

Often, we assume that if we really had it together and could approach God without sin, without failing, with only our pure spiritual successes to offer, then God would somehow delight in our prayer more. The opposite is true. If you approach God in that manner, you approach Him as one opposed to Him, for we are all fallen. If we presume to approach Him as more than needy, dependent sons and daughters, God rightly takes offense. There's nothing more dangerous than the pride of devotional consistency.

Grace is for God's People

That's a real shocker, right? This grace is for you right now—now and tonight and tomorrow and next week and forever. The deadly assumption made too often among those who claim to heed the Scriptures is that *grace is only for non-Christians*. Grace is what God offers to people who don't know Christ. Grace is what makes us Christians; but once we're Christians, we live by our own resources. There are some among us who really do believe that God offers grace to *unbelievers* who will turn to God through Jesus Christ. And they're right on that. What they wrongly assume, though, is that the Christian life begins by grace, but continues by human works.

This assumption—that grace isn't for Christians—is spiritual venom, which is keeping millions of Christians in bondage to self-reliance, guilt, shame, and despair. Quiet Time Guilt is the great epidemic among Bible-believing Christians today.

If you think the purpose behind this chapter is to absolve you from the call to pray or the need for Scripture, think again. My purpose is to lead you to grasp the freedom which comes only through Christ.

Freedom is Found in Desiring God

My hope is that you will find freedom from the desire to pray and move into freedom for the desire of God; from the desire of Bible study to the desire of God Himself; and from the desire for a quiet time to a desire for Jesus.

A. B. Simpson said it so well many years ago when he penned the lyrics to a time-tested hymn, entitled "Himself:"

> *Once it was the blessing, Now it is the Lord;*
> *Once it was the feeling, Now it is His Word.*
> *Once His gifts I wanted, Now the Giver own;*
> *Once I sought for healing, Now Himself alone.*
> *Once it was my working, His it hence shall be;*
> *Once I tried to use Him, Now He uses me;*
> *Once the pow'r I wanted, Now the Mighty One;*

Once for self I labored, Now for Him alone.
All in all forever,
Jesus will I sing;
Everything in Jesus,
And Jesus everything.[4]

I long for you to luxuriate in the pure message of the gospel, spelled out on page after page of the Bible, and to find the joyous freedom found in Christ. Prayer is a grace, not a work. It is a confession of our neediness to God, not a proof that our "relationship with God" is going well.

If you think that God will not bless you today because you missed your quiet time, this has been for you. If subtle legalism has left you in bondage so that you no longer hunger for God's Word or freely call out to Him in prayer, then please hear this: as His child, God has already chosen you, pronounced you righteous, adopted you into His family, and promised to finish His work in you.

Perhaps you have been lied to in the past. Now it is time for the truth to set you free. Free to be needy. Free to fail. Free to approach God without dread. Free to delight in Him rather than in your performance.

Imagine for a moment you're meeting a fellow Christ-follower, and he/she asks you, "How's your relationship with God going?" And you answer, "Well, I'm struggling with my attitude about my job—but God is teaching me to be content and to not gossip when people rub me the wrong way." A silent stare greets the words, your inquisitor's eyes staring you up and down. After a moment of awkward silence, the question comes again, "But how is your relationship with God?" Hmm. What's wrong with this picture?

You see, in the minds of many, the sum total of my relationship with God is my devotional consistency. Your quiet time, however, does not define your relationship with God. Your relationship with Him—or, perhaps we should say, God's relationship with you—is your whole life: your job, your family, your sleep, your play, your relationships, your driving, your everything. The real irony here is that we've become accustomed to pigeonholing our entire relationship with God into a brief devotional exercise that is not even commanded in the Bible.

The daily quiet time—that bell-induced 6:40 to 7:10 a.m. half-hour every day of Scriptural study and prayer I experienced—is not actually commanded in the Bible. Binding the conscience where Scripture allows freedom is a very, very serious crime. Legalism is rearing its ugly, fat head again.

Please don't misunderstand what I'm saying. My goal isn't that we pray and read the Bible less, but that we do so more—but with a free and needy heart.

Does the Bible instruct Christians to call out to God in prayer? Absolutely. The apostle Paul exhorts us, "*Rejoice always; pray without ceasing; in everything give thanks; for this is God's will for you in Christ Jesus.*"[5] Yet this isn't a command to set apart a special half-hour of prayer; it's instruction to continually call upon God.

Paul also writes:

> Be anxious for nothing, but in everything by prayer and supplication with thanksgiving let your requests be made known to God. And the peace of God, which surpasses all comprehension, will guard your hearts and your minds in Christ Jesus.[6]

Notice, however, that the focus here is not on the performance of a devotional duty, but on approaching God for grace—for our hearts and minds to be guarded by Him. Paul's burden is that we would rely upon God in every circumstance and therefore have peace, rather than relying on ourselves and finding ourselves captive to the anxiety that accompanies self-reliance.

Is the Pre-Sunrise, Morning Devotional Optional? Yes.

Does the Bible command us to read our Bibles every day? Not really, no. What Scripture actually instructs is that we meditate on God's Word all the time. Consider the godly man in Psalm 1: *"But his delight is in the law of the LORD, and in His law he meditates day and night."*[7] This is not exactly the same thing as reading the Bible every day. Personal Bible reading is one—and only one—way we meditate upon God's Word.

At this point it's helpful to consider the difference between a good idea and a biblical mandate. A biblical mandate is something that God explicitly or implicitly commands in Scripture. Loving your neighbor is a biblical mandate (Matthew 5:43). Moving to a city to work in a homeless shelter, by contrast, is not a biblical mandate. It might be a good idea—a wonderful possible application of the biblical mandate to love your neighbor. But moving to a city isn't the only way you can love your neighbor. Similarly, meditating on God's Word is a biblical mandate. The daily quiet time, by contrast, is a good idea— a wonderful possible application of the mandate of biblical meditation.

It may surprise you to know that the concept of quiet time as a command is a fairly modern invention. It's only in recent centuries that Christians have been able to actually own Bibles—the printing press and cheap paper (and now the internet) have given us more options so far as biblical meditation is concerned. *Remember, however, that most Christians throughout history have not owned Bibles.* They heard the Bible preached during corporate worship. They were taught the Bible in the churches. They memorized the Bible profusely. But for most Christians throughout history, biblical meditation took place when they discussed the Bible with family and friends, when they memorized it, and when they listened very carefully to God's Word preached. The concept of sitting still before sunrise with a Bible open would have been very foreign to them.

We have so many options today, so why get hung up on a regimented, early morning quiet time if that isn't your cup of tea? Listen to Christian teaching CDs or podcasts. Invest your time in a small group Bible study. Have friends over for coffee and Bible discussion. Sing and listen to Scripture songs. Read good theology. Tape memory verses to the dashboard of your car. Pray throughout your day. I always reserve the drive to church on Sundays as a time of uninterrupted prayer for the people I pastor, for the preaching of God's Word, for those leading worship, and for the peace and purity of the church. Certain landmarks around town remind me to pray for certain churches, Christians I know, or causes God says are important. I often spend more time praying in my pickup truck than on my knees.

I have a morning quiet time. Why? It works for me. If you have a regular quiet time—morning, noon, or night—please don't stop. You've found a wonderful way to meditate on Scripture. Perhaps you'd like to set aside a specific time to call upon God in prayer, but if the thought of that at 5:45 a.m. doesn't work for you, that's okay. You should not feel guilty because you have not broken a commandment. A quiet time is an option, a good idea—not a biblical mandate.

If the idea of some time alone with God every morning is foreign to you, and you can't imagine yourself doing that right now, there are other good options. The key is to rely on God to accomplish His plans, a reliance expressed in prayer and fed in Scripture. You have all kinds of opportunities to call upon God in prayer and to meditate upon His Word. He loves you and delights in your expressions of weakness and dependence. He is glorified in your weakness.

Many early African converts to Christianity were earnest and regular in their private devotions. In some tribal settings, each person reportedly had a separate spot in the thicket where he or she would pour out their hearts to God. Over time the paths to these places became well worn. As a result, if one of the believers began to neglect prayer, it was soon apparent to the others. They would kindly remind the negligent one, "*Brother, the grass grows on your path.*"[8]

Whenever and however you spend time with your Lord Jesus, may the grass never grow over your path.

CHAPTER NINE

Prayer:

Communicating with God

I am a history buff and enjoy reading biographies and stories of the great men and women of the past. (I've always been of the mind that we would be foolish not to learn from other people who have been through experiences similar to ours.) I cannot count the times, as I have read accounts of soldiers—particularly from America's Civil War—who had been cut down and wounded on the battlefield, who instinctively and immediately cried out for their mothers. They were perhaps the manliest of men in the barracks and amongst the other soldiers; but, when they were hurting and facing imminent death, they immediately sought help from the person nearest and dearest to their heart.

That is the natural outcome of the most tender relationship possible between a parent and child. Those same soldiers, strong and virile, who perhaps had many times playfully lifted Mother up and carried her around the kitchen laughing and joking, were now calling for her with the heart of a child for the comfort that only a mother could give.

That, my friend, is illustrative of prayer at its richest and first impulse. It is reaching up with the hands of a newborn spiritual child to the great God, who is both Father and Mother. God, revealed to us in the Living and written Word, is whose name we whisper every time we pray and say, "*Our Father in heaven . . .*"

In this chapter, we are not going to deal with the problems and obstacles of prayer or the need of prayer, but with the practice of prayer. A person may be very wise and clever in dealing with problems but may know nothing of the practice. A person might be a deep thinker, without being a wise practitioner. There isn't much of a mystery about it, as some people seem to think: prayer is simply the natural outcome of a relationship with Jesus Christ.

Now that you have entered into a relationship with God through His Son Jesus Christ, that relationship, now established, must be maintained. Any relationship, when it is loving, close, and endearing relies on communication. In a home, if relationships are normal, you can count on it that there is good communication happening between the family members. Children who love to be with Mom and Dad will naturally cry out for them when they are in trouble; and, just as naturally, their cries generally bring immediate help.

The Practice of Prayer

You will never prove prayer by arguments. It is only proven in practice. Once you have lived a life of prayer as your daily habit, no persuasive argument will ever move you. The sneers and scorn of others, and the explanations of cultured people using psychological language seeking to disprove the reality of what you now believe in, will sound to you like the babbling of fools. You will have proven prayer in your own life and will also realize that the ones speaking to you about prayer know absolutely nothing about it.

The first impulse of a newly converted soul is to pray as much as the first act of a newly born child is to cry. Making prayer a part of your daily life will eventually be as essential to you as breathing. The follower of Jesus who neglects prayer or allows prayer to slip into a "once-in-a-blue-moon" regularity is committing spiritual suicide. It's no different than if a person allowed himself to be placed in a vacuum without any access to oxygen.

A Beautiful Relationship

Author Lionel Fletcher reminds us that one of the saddest places to visit as a guest is the home where the children are allowed the run of the place, where they treat it like a motel and not a home. They come and go as they please, expecting to be waited on hand and foot. When they speak, it's only about what they want or need or to find fault because something is not the way they want it to be. They walk into the kitchen every day without so much as a "good morning!" and stalk off to bed at night without a word. Their parents often don't know where they are, rarely share in the enjoyments of life, have no idea of each other's experiences of the day; and, the kids, when asked about their day, resent being asked and tell the parents to butt out of their business.[1]

Contrast that home with the one where, on entering, Mom or Dad are swarmed by the children. The smallest ones are lifted up and flung high in the air, squealing with delight. The older ones are met with embraces. At the end of the day, there are hugs and kisses and faithful parental promises to come tuck them in when the little ones call. Once called, Mom and Dad make their rounds, listening to the replayed events of the day, with bursts of giggling over some tickling, capped off with a story and a good night prayer.

That is a picture of a beautiful family relationship enriched by loving parents who point their children to God. And what is that but an example of the Christian life? God, our wonderful Father, the Creator and Controller of the universe, yet as the prophet Isaiah reminds us, is as kindhearted as the tenderest mother bird.[2]

Our Father is waiting to hear our cry, anxious to supply our need, so loving and caring toward us that His blessings are only limited by our willingness to receive them. It is a perfect relationship made possible through the life and sacrifice of Jesus, if we will only take advantage of it.

Jesus' Example

Jesus Himself taught us how to pray. Most of us are familiar with the Lord's Prayer, *"Our Father who is in heaven . . ."*[3] This prayer is recorded twice in the Gospels—in Matthew 6 and in Luke 11. I am of the conviction that Jesus was not intending to give the disciples some sort of prayer that they could memorize and then just deliver back to heaven. It's much deeper than that. Jesus wanted to give His followers a model to follow when addressing God, so we can learn how to pray like Jesus prayed. Let's take a look at how Jesus teaches us to pray.

Address God as Father

"Our Father, who is in heaven . . ."[4]

Jesus said, *"Pray, then, in this way say, 'Our Father.'"* His Father is our Father. This thought, which Jesus places first in His instructions regarding prayer, at the outset reveals relationship and shows us that, *"The Lord is like a father to his children, tender and compassionate to those who fear him."*[5] When I was a new father, I found sheer delight in listening to the babbling sounds of our infant daughters. Similarly, our Father in heaven loves to hear us speaking to Him about the smallest details of our lives.

Address God as Holy

"Hallowed be your name . . ."

This always reminds me of the little girl who came home from church one day and told her mom that she now knew God's first name.

Momma said, "Excuse me? I didn't know God had a first name."

The little girl replied, "He sure does. It's 'Howard.'"

Mom was sort of stunned—she was pretty sure God wasn't really named Howard. So, she asked, "Darling, where did you hear that?"

The little girl said, "At church today. They taught us to pray, 'Our Father who is in heaven, Howard be your name.'"

"Hallowed" comes from the English word "holy." Why does Jesus include the concept of "hallowed"? Because without it, our understanding of "Father" can be distorted—it could become sentimental to the point of presuming upon and taking advantage of the Father's graciousness towards us. "Hallowed" reminds us that the Father is holy, set apart from sin. Including "hallowed be your name" in our prayers means that we are to approach our heavenly Father, not with presumptive familiarity but with reverence and respect for his greatness and holiness. He is our "Dad," but He is also Holy. And as we are learning to pray, we must not forget this. Jesus is reminding us that God our Father is, "Daddy, Sir."

Address God as Coming King

"Your kingdom come. Your will be done, on earth as it is in Heaven."

The kingdom of God comes when Jesus proclaims God's reign and demonstrates that reign by preaching good news to the poor, freedom for the spiritually imprisoned, sight for the blind, release for the oppressed, and the Jubilee Day of the Lord.[6] The kingdom is here in Jesus and His disciples—and in you and me—but it will come fully and completely when He returns to earth to reign over all as King and Lord.[7]

When we pray, "Your kingdom come," we are asking God to manifest the power and glory of His kingdom in us and throughout our world. What a prayer! We are praying that Christ might reign over all. We are also asking the Father to hasten the return of Jesus Christ to this earth!

Address God as your Provider

"Give us this day our daily bread."

The words used in this phrase are very rare words in the Greek language. For example, the word "daily" is found only in this verse in the entire Bible. It isn't even a word used in the secular, classical Greek language of the day. *Vine's Expository Dictionary* says that, "the prayer is to be for bread that suffices for this day and next, so that the mind may conform to Christ's warning against anxiety for the morrow."[8]

It's strange, but we long to break free from the necessity of praying this prayer. We would like to store up enough money or food so that we don't have to worry—or pray—about where our next meal will come from. We would like to be "comfortably" well off, if not rich.

I'm not saying that Jesus wants every believer to be poverty-stricken, though if that were to happen to us, He is able to meet our needs. He does, however, want us to get in the habit of relying upon the Father—for everything. Jesus is teaching us to look to the Father for every provision. He is interested in your job. He is concerned about the health of your business. He cares about your school. He cares about your marriage, your children, and your relationships.

Address God as your Forgiver

"And forgive us our debts, as we also have forgiven our debtors."

The word "debt" here should be understood as sin. Sin describes a broken relationship, a breach of trust, an ugly deed, a selfish value system. This petition of the Lord's Prayer requires a recognition of the need for forgiveness. Not just forgiveness once in our lives, but continual forgiveness. Yes, as we follow Jesus, sin's hold over us loosens; but there still is sin we need to take seriously.

Not only is forgiveness for us to receive, but also to be offered. Jesus teaches us to pray, "Forgive us . . . because we also forgive." Is our forgiveness dependent upon us forgiving? When you read Jesus' explanation of the Lord's Prayer in Matthew 6:14-15, you'd certainly think so: *"For if you forgive other people when they sin against you, your heavenly Father will also forgive you. But if you do not forgive others their sins, your Father will not forgive your sins."*[9]

But, having said that, there is no way that we can earn forgiveness by amassing "forgiveness points" by forgiving others. Forgiveness is by God's grace through Jesus' atonement for our sins, not by any merit we have. Yet, unforgiveness can block God's blessing. D. L. Moody, said, "I firmly believe a great many prayers are not answered because we are not willing to forgive someone."[10]

Address God as your Guide

"And do not lead us into temptation . . ."

Does God tempt us? No. In James 1:13-15, Jesus' half-brother, the apostle James, teaches us:

> *When tempted, no one should say, "God is tempting me." For God cannot be tempted by evil, nor does he tempt anyone; but each person is tempted when they are dragged away by their own evil desire and enticed.*

Then, after desire has conceived, it gives birth to sin; and sin, when it is full-grown, gives birth to death.[11]

Far from tempting us, Christians believe that God guides our steps. This is a prayer that God would protect us against temptation. Then Jesus adds the phrase, *"but deliver us from evil"* or *"deliver us from the evil one."* Jesus is teaching us to be dependent upon God to help us in times of temptation, when the tempter seems especially strong. We can pray, "Don't lead me into places where I can be tempted, I pray, but lead me in places where You are and where I can be free."

Address God as the One Who Rules Over All Things

"For Yours is the kingdom and the power and the glory forever. Amen."

All things are from God. For the Lord, all things exist and were created. To God belongs all the praise, honor, and glory. We are His people and the sheep of His pasture. All the means for accomplishing His will are done through His power, His kingdom, and His glorious purposes. The rule of God is the goal of our prayer.

Jesus ends the prayer with an *"Amen."* Do you know what that word means? We tack it on the end of a prayer without really thinking about it. "Amen" has different meanings throughout Scripture, but in this case, in the context of this prayer, the underlying meaning of the word "Amen" is "truth." It is a solemn affirmation. When we say "Amen," we are saying, "Yes, before God I agree with that, I believe that to be true, I want that to be so."

God Answers Prayer

The greatest Scriptural proof you need concerning prayer will be found when you begin to familiarize yourself with the Bible. You will find that the great heroes and heroines of the faith were all people of prayer. You will discover that Jesus was a man of prayer and that He prayed for us even on the cross. Therefore, you know that you can, should, and must pray, but you need to rid yourself of the notion that prayer is nothing more than bringing a laundry list of wants to God on a daily basis. We tend to limit prayer to asking. Theologians call that type of prayer "petition," and it certainly has its place in prayer; but no one would like their child to only speak when asking for things.

Remember, too, that God hears and answers every prayer. Don't make the dreadful mistake, however, of assuming that prayers are only answered when there is a "yes" from heaven. If God grants what is asked, only then do some say that God answered their prayer. That is far from correct. In that case, God has answered their prayer through His consent, but He answers every prayer, whether or not He has granted His consent.

A child may see some liquid in a pretty colored bottle and ask for it, only to have his mother protectively answer, "No, no." The liquid, known to the mother, is harmful. She will lovingly give her child something equally pretty and something even better. Every Christian who has walked with God for a long time, in looking back over his or her life, can thank God in all sincerity for the prayers He did not answer the way they thought they wanted Him to; and, they will say, along with the apostle Paul, *"And we know that all things work together for good to those who love God . . ."*[12] They might also agree with country music star, Garth Brooks, when he sang, "Sometimes I thank God for unanswered prayers"![13]

Share your joys and victories with the Lord. Thank Him for the blessings in your life and of the day. Tell Him all of your plans, your hopes, your dreams. Then ask Him to overrule all of your ideas as well as your ambitions if they are going to inadvertently lead you away from Him. Take time to adore, praise, and worship Him. Pray for others. Don't just pray for the things that line up with your own will but pray that His will would be accomplished in your life. Your Christian life can never reach maturity and its richest development until you realize that the epitome of a Christian's life is that God's will is having its uninterrupted way.

Set a Time for Prayer

One of the most challenging commands in the entire Bible is found in the book of 1 Thessalonians: *"Pray without ceasing."*[14] How in the world do we obey a command like that? There are various ways, but without a system of some sort, I think we will be very challenged to fulfill this call. By a system, I mean having a set time of prayer. It is not enough to pray when you fall out of bed in the morning or when you are drifting off to sleep at day's end to just bow your knee and pray a few rote prayers. These are wonderful things to do, and I think it ought to be our practice to pray in the morning and evening. But there should be some time set aside when you are at your best.

I have known a number of people through the years who not only take time in the morning and evening for prayer, but they find time for communion with God in the middle of the day, usually around their lunch hour. Finding a time in the middle of the day to refocus on Him, to bring your heart and needs before Him, to praise and worship, is an excellent habit. Some people take a walk and pray. Others might sit in their car during lunch. The key is to find a quiet place without interruption.

So, make prayer the practice of your life. And if you find that something is interrupting it or that you are getting out of the habit of prayer, then you must take yourself in hand, and with a prayer for help, bring yourself back to what will very soon again become a daily act of delight.

CHAPTER TEN

Sharing Your Faith:
Telling Others about Christ

The Search for Delicious by Natalie Babbitt is a 1969 novel written with children in mind.[1] As with many wonderful stories with staying power, there are lessons in it for everyone.

The Prime Minister of the land embarks upon a large-scale project: the compilation of a dictionary. Instead of simply defining the words as one might expect, the dictionary instead provides examples of words. When brought to the King and Queen for approval, they are happy with, "Affectionate is your dog," and, "Bulky is a big bag of boxes," and, "Calamitous is saying 'no' to the King," but they take issue with, "Delicious is fried fish." No, says the King; fried fish is not delicious in the least. It's apples. No, says the Queen; it's Christmas pudding. No, says the Queen's brother; it's nuts—and he storms out of the castle. A general declares that beer is delicious.

With no agreement in sight, the King sends the Prime Minister's special assistant, a twelve-year-old lad named Galen, to travel the length and breadth of the kingdom and poll the people as to what they consider delicious. The King announces that whatever food or drink receives the most votes will go into the dictionary.

Excitedly, Galen grasped the reins of his kingly commission and off he went. He quickly discovered, however, that his task was becoming impossible. No one in the land could agree on anything; neighbors and friends ridiculed one another's choices and championed their own. It all went precipitously downhill, to such an extent that it soon looked inevitable that civil war would break out.

An uprising like this obviously left the King very vulnerable, and seeing this, an evil opponent attempted a takeover of the kingdom by damming up the country's freshwater supply, further alienating the people from their leader. The story excitedly twists and turns leading to Galen saving the day, along with Ardis, a mermaid who was the guardian of the freshwater spring. When at last the water began flowing again, the parched people drank greedily and deeply, proclaiming the cool spring water was, "delicious, yes, yes, delicious!" The King finally had his definition.

If you and I were asked to give examples of what we find delicious, I suspect we would be like those in the story: we would probably have differing opinions. If we, however, experienced the dread of a famine, it is likely we would declare that even a morsel of bread to be delicious. Jesus Himself told us that He is the bread of life.[2] As a new Christian you have, as the Psalmist said, tasted and have seen that the Lord is good.[3]

The world offers us much in the form of taste but always leaves us hungry and empty. Having tasted what Jesus offers, you have discovered the only One who can meet your need. You have been thirsty and discovered living water. What should be our response to that?

Thankfulness to God immediately springs to mind, first and foremost. On its heels, those of us who have been beggars must tell other beggars where to find the bread!

The Greatest Adventure

From the outset, I encourage new believers to break free from the smug idea our society has regarding what is and is not correct regarding religion. That is, "we mustn't speak of religion or politics." I tend to agree with the famed British author, G. K. Chesterton, who said, "I never discuss anything except politics and religion. There is nothing else to discuss!"

To imagine that a person, whose life has been radically transformed by the Savior of the world, shouldn't speak about that transaction is nothing short of an attempt by Satan to paralyze the church of God, and, to a very large extent, he has been successful. You should resist this, not by some over-the-top, boorish manner of sharing your faith, but with all courtesy and passion take your stand as a follower of Jesus Christ, so that He might, through you, captivate those who have not yet met Him.

Every Christian is called to be a missionary, and by that word I don't mean what we call a foreign missionary. That said, I believe that every child of God should be ready and available to serve the Lord overseas if and when called. It is a good thing for us if we always bear in mind the command Jesus left us when He said:

"Go therefore and make disciples of all the nations, baptizing them in the name of the Father and the Son and the Holy Spirit, teaching them to observe all that I commanded you; and lo, I am with you always, even to the end of the age."[4]

No argument can stand up against that. Every Christ-follower should determine from the outset of their personal relationship with Jesus to go out into their world as a preacher and proclaimer of the gospel, in whatever form that might take.

If you get that tremendous adventure for Christ into your heart, mind, and soul, it will keep you out of the rut in which too many Christians find themselves. And, once in a rut, it won't be long before you realize it has turned into a grave.

You have been bought with a price and won over by Jesus Christ. You have accepted His gift of everlasting life. You have been born again into God's kingdom and now, you are not only an heir, you are a joint heir with Jesus Christ. You subscribe to the astounding fact that you are a child of the Most High God! What use is it, then, for you to say you believe all of this if you never act on any of it?

Again, this does not mean that you should incessantly intrude your beliefs upon others. No, not at all. It does mean, however, that wherever you may find yourself in the world and no matter what you may find yourself doing there, that you realize God has you there for a special purpose and reason. He has a special work for you to do in that place. It begins with telling others about Him.

Telling Your Story

So how do you tell others about Jesus? In the New Testament book of Acts, in chapter 21, we discover that Paul had been falsely accused of bringing a Gentile inside the Jewish temple, where Gentiles were not allowed to go. A riot erupted. Paul was forcibly pulled out of the temple, then beaten by the crowd until a captain of the Roman Guard broke it up, arrested Paul, and bound him in chains. Paul then asked the captain for an opportunity to speak to the crowd, and surprisingly, the captain agreed. In chapter 22, Paul gave his personal testimony. In other words, he told his story, and we can follow his example. Here's how he did it.

Establish common ground.

Paul began relating his personal experience by finding common ground with those who wanted his head on a platter:

> *"Brothers and fathers, listen now to my defense." When they heard him speak to them in Aramaic, they became very quiet. Then Paul said: "I am a Jew, born in Tarsus of Cilicia, but brought up in this city. I studied under Gamaliel and was thoroughly trained in the law of our ancestors. I was just as zealous for God as any of you are today."*[5]

Paul begins by telling them that he was once just like them. He addressed them as brothers, and he spoke to them in their native language. Strong common threads are the basis for any meaningful relationship. Find things in common with those you want to introduce to Christ. The list of commonalities is seemingly endless: children, background, favorite teams, jobs, education, food, shopping, sports, hobbies, clothing, books. When you do this, you will begin to build rapport, and then you can begin to build a relationship, and a relationship can build into a friendship. Next . . .

Avoid glorifying your past life of sin.

Paul tells of his past, but he does not glory in it:

> *"I persecuted the followers of this Way to their death, arresting both men and women and throwing them into prison, as the high priest and all the Council can themselves testify. I even obtained letters from them to their associates in Damascus and went there to bring these people as prisoners to Jerusalem to be punished."*[6]

I think what Paul is teaching us here is that we can acknowledge our life before Jesus took over, but we do not need to revel in it.

Avoid promising a life of ease to those who believe.

Paul tells his listeners that being saved by Jesus changed his life, but he does not tell them that things have always been great since he was saved (after all, he is saying this with new bruises). He did not say, "I just wanted to tell you how the Lord has blessed me materially. My tent-making business has never been better." Be honest, be real, be authentic. Tell it like it is.

Remember that as you demonstrate Christ in you, people are more willing to listen to what Jesus can do in them.

Not every conversion story is as dramatic as Paul's, but every testimony is a "before and after" account of the transformation of a human life by Jesus Christ. Paul described the man that he was and the man that Christ had enabled to him to be. He was not saying how good he was or what he had done, but how good Jesus was and what He had done. Throughout his speech, Paul clarified that it was Jesus who had changed him. In verse six, he said:

> *"About noon as I came near Damascus, suddenly a bright light from heaven flashed around me. I fell to the ground and heard a voice say to me, 'Saul! Saul! Why do you persecute me?'*
>
> *"'Who are you, Lord?' I asked.*
>
> *"'I am Jesus of Nazareth, whom you are persecuting' he replied. My companions saw the light, but they did not understand the voice of him who was speaking to me.*
>
> *"'What shall I do, Lord?' I asked.*
>
> *"'Get up,' the Lord said, 'and go into Damascus. There you will be told all that you have been assigned to do.'"*[7]

Paul's life displayed the changes that had been made in his life and so should ours.

Present your conversion to following Jesus as a fact, not a feeling.

Paul's story was based on verifiable facts—things to which others could attest, not just how he felt.

> "My companions led me by the hand into Damascus, because the brilliance of the light had blinded me.
>
> "A man named Ananias came to see me. He was a devout observer of the law and highly respected by all the Jews living there. He stood beside me and said, 'Brother Saul, receive your sight!' And at that very moment I was able to see him.
>
> "Then he said: 'The God of our fathers has chosen you to know his will and to see the Righteous One and to hear words from his mouth. You will be his witness to all men of what you have seen and heard. And now what are you waiting for? Get up, be baptized and wash your sins away, calling on his name.'"[8]

Open and Shut

Every Christian is to give himself or herself to the work of the Lord, and then leave it entirely up to the Holy Spirit to close or open doors of conversation and opportunity as He so chooses. He knows your giftedness, your heart, your abilities, your personality type, and what life experiences you have had. He will coalesce all of those things in service of the gospel.

Many new believers decide immediately to begin sharing their new faith with everyone that they can, but a very small proportion continue that for a lifetime. Nevertheless, I am convinced that the first impulse of the newborn soul to tell others about Jesus Christ is absolutely the correct one. It isn't for you and me, therefore, to say we won't share with others; it is for us to say, "I will share my faith in Jesus with so-and-so unless God shuts the door and opens another path to me."

We can only serve to the degree that we are equipped; therefore, when we are completely given over to the control of God's Holy Spirit, we will be placed in the right environments—at the right place and at the right time. This may be in your hometown or in another nation. One thing you should decide though: will you be a champion of the Cross, proclaiming the gospel of Jesus everywhere you go?

We all know that the best way to learn how to do anything is to attempt to do it. This is true of a butcher, baker, and candlestick maker, and it is true of service to Christ. No one can become a mechanic unless they are willing to get their hands dirty, learn how to operate the tools, and understand the basics of how a combustion engine works. You will learn by mistakes and by practice, and it is always encouraging at how proficiency follows practice. One of the most fulfilling things you can experience as a Christ-follower is when God calls you to more challenging assignments after you have completed the task at hand.

We are in a battle—the Bible calls it a spiritual war—and there can never be any question of retirement or looking for the easy way of doing things. We must give over our faculties to the power and control of the Holy Spirit. The Christian who is looking for easy posts, soft positions, and unchallenging steps of faith has already lost the zeal and fire of those first days of encounter with Jesus. When those things occur, our spiritual self degenerates, our vision begins to fade, and the immediate and physical become more important than our service to Christ and His gospel.

Time and again through thirty-five years in Christian ministry, I have listened intently to stories from people who have become followers of Christ, and they trace their interest in Jesus and their submission to the gospel to the consistent witnessing and service of a friend or family member. They heard and saw the love of Jesus with word and deed, with gentleness and respect,[9] and a once proud, independent person bowed the knee at the foot of the Cross.

Wherever you go, you will find doors open to you. Since you are now a child of God, you must be about your Father's business, and you must leave it to your heavenly Father's wisdom to guide your footsteps and activities. He cannot guide you, however, until you are actively at work, doing whatever He has called you to with all of your might. Remember, after all, it's much easier to steer a moving car than one which is parked!

Doing the Work Within Our Reach

On February 3, 1943, during the height of the Second World War, a troop ship named the *Dorchester* was carrying more than 900 soldiers and military personnel across the North Atlantic Ocean. A German U-boat spotted the convoy and fired three torpedoes at the ship. Only one struck the target, but the blast below the waterline fatally damaged the ship. In the cold darkness, the crew was ordered to abandon ship. There were not enough lifeboats for all the men, nor were there enough life jackets.

Four chaplains aboard the ship that night helped comfort those injured in the explosion and those who feared the coming of death. When it appeared that the ship was ready to sink, the chaplains took off their life jackets and handed them to four young soldiers who had none. They gave up their own lives in order to save others. The heroic gesture inspired a nation, and Congress voted a special posthumous medal in their honor.[10]

Like the chaplains, our role as followers of Jesus is to do the work immediately within our reach, in our own spheres of influence, and tell others of Christ. They were praying with those in danger and telling them of God's saving grace. When we have proven to Him our sincerity, integrity, and capacity, He will then call us to go deeper and wider. And that, my friend, is "delicious, yes, yes, delicious!"

ADDENDUM

Knowing and Loving God's Word

This is not about studying the Bible in a systematic way, nor is it intended to address deep theological questions which would be posed to a student studying for the ministry. We will look into the question of just how someone who is beginning their brand-new Christian life can find enrichment for their minds and hearts by daily reading and studying God's Word, the Bible.

One of the marks of a person whose life has truly been transformed by Jesus is a hunger for His Word. This is the work of the Holy Spirit, who moves this newly born life to seek and find soul nourishment. In nature, God works in amazing ways to provide food for helpless, newly born animals, and in providing them with innate impulses which they follow, they find nourishment for their life and growth.

For example, let's consider a truly incredible creature: the kangaroo! At full adulthood, some can reach a height of seven feet. And yet, just coming into the world as newborns, baby kangaroos are some of the most tiny, helpless creatures you can imagine. They are just a few inches in length at birth, devoid of hair, and blind as a bat. How do they find their way into their mother's pouch where there is warmth, nourishment, and protection awaiting them, and where they are to be carried and fed for their first few months on this planet?

Just after they are born, kangaroos immediately begin to climb up their mother's fur, clinging on by their tiny claws, until they reach the pouch, where they drop and find everything they need.

How can a blind, little object no longer than a person's thumb know where its mother's pouch is? How can it possibly know there is milk and warmth and safety there? Why does it not wander off in a different direction to certain death?

We could ask the same questions about a seed which drops from a plant to the ground. Yet we know that when the roots come from the seed, they go downward into the moisture, and the shoot goes up into the light and air. If you take one of those seeds from the cradle of the earth after it has begun to shoot, and turn it upside down so that the shoot will point down and the roots point up, cover it up with earth again and leave it, the roots will turn over and go down, and the shoot will twist itself and go up, each to its proper environment.

But why?

The answer is a simple one: God provides for all new life. It is His desire that all creatures of His love might live and fulfill their purpose.

If He does all of that for the kangaroo and a plant, how much more will He provide for the newborn soul? "You must be born again," said Jesus, and when we are born again, the Holy Spirit leads us to nourishment and a hunger comes upon us for the Bible, God's Word.

The Bible: God's Holy Book

When I take God's Holy Book into my hands, I am always amazed at how, during the epochs and ages, it has been created, compiled, and protected. It remains today as packed full of value as it ever was. Do not allow any doubt to enter your mind about that.

In over 2,000 years since Jesus walked this earth, generations have thought that the Bible would soon pass away, that its value had been undermined, that its revelation had been proved spurious, but today there are more Bibles disseminated—in print and electronically—than ever before in the history of the world. It never is old-fashioned or out of date. Its literature can be read and appreciated today as much as 2,000 years ago. There is no other book under the sun about which this is true.

Charles Haddon Spurgeon preached to tens of thousands during the nineteenth century from his pulpit in London, England, and yet his sermons are read mostly by theologians and preachers today. Sermons which shook the multitudes 100 years ago can be tiresome and difficult to read today. But the Bible is as fresh, as glorious, and as convincing as it ever was because it is still the Word of God, and it leads people to salvation. It will lead every newborn soul into an enriched Christian life, if the person will only take it and use it for spiritual nourishment.

Be careful, therefore, in your new Christian life, to sense and obey the leading of the Holy Spirit. You will find yourself longing to know the Bible and how to pray. These are leadings you must follow because without Bible study and prayer as a regular discipline of your daily life, you will never become a strong Christian.

I can say without any hesitation, in three-and-a-half decades of Christian ministry, that whenever I have had someone come to me who had admittedly fallen away from the faith, one of the first things they will admit to is a falling away from prayer and Bible study. It can happen to anyone of us, yet if we will diligently study and read God's Word and cultivate a prayer life, we will stay strong and connected to our heavenly Father.

You are being led right now, in these early days of your faith, by the Holy Spirit to living water and the bread of life. Eat and drink as regularly as you would take meals for your bodily sustenance.

I think there are three good and valuable tools for a new Christian to possess: a Bible in a trustworthy and understandable translation, a concordance, and a commentary.

Finding a Good Bible

Beginning with the Bible, I would advise you, even if you have to go without a new pair of shoes or food, to buy a well-bound, leather-covered edition. It will be your life-long companion. Find one of which you like the appearance and the feel. Purchase the best copy you can afford. As a pastor, I own many copies of varying value and different translations, but I have one Bible that is my constant companion. I have used it regularly since 1979, and

I plan to have it until I die, at which point it will pass on to my family.

I will also say, that if I could have only one Bible, it would be the Zondervan New American Standard (translation) Study Bible (NASB). It possesses an excellent system of side-margin references that help you understand the text at hand, as well as wonderful explanations and commentary of the majority of Bible verses. Here are a few other reasons why I recommend this translation:

1. The strength for me of the NASB is its literalness. More so than any other English Bible translation, the NASB seeks to take what was originally said in Hebrew, Aramaic, and Greek and say the same thing in English.

2. The NASB footnotes and side-margin references have been praised by many for being extremely helpful.

3. It is a readily available translation, easily found online and at most any bookstore.

4. It is quite readable (the 1995 edition removed some of the archaic "Thee's" and "Thou's" from earlier editions).

5. It, unlike newer "gender-inclusive" translations, maintains proper pronouns for God, men, and women, if those were written by the original biblical authors.

Finding a Concordance

Let's get the first question about a concordance out of the way: What in the world is a concordance?

A concordance can be a great tool to help you in studying the Bible. It contains an alphabetical index of words used in Scripture and the references in the Bible where the word occurs.

Have you ever half-recalled a Bible verse but couldn't remember it in its entirety or where it is located? If you can recall a main word, then a concordance is your answer. For example, you may have heard it said that money is the root of all evil, but something about that doesn't sit right with you. You can look up the word money, and a concordance will tell you all the places that word is found in the Bible, usually with a portion of the verse. You scan down, find the passage you're searching for, then look up the verse, and your hunch is correct: the Bible never said that. It does say that the love of money is the root of all evil. And you have become a better-informed student of God's Word.

Most good Bibles will contain a concordance in the back of the Bible (the NASB Study Bible I recommended above contains a very good concordance). Be aware that concordances are translation specific. A concordance geared to the King James Version may not be too helpful with an NASB or an English Standard Version. Several concordances are found online and are available for free. You can also buy concordance books.

Finding a Commentary

A Bible commentary explains the biblical text by someone (usually a scholar) who has immersed himself or herself in the original language, context, and form of biblical texts. The Bible commentator delivers to us details that we simply don't have by the simple reading of Scripture, like archaeological discoveries, historical details, linguistic particularities, and details about geography and culture.

There is a big difference between one-volume commentaries on the whole Bible, which naturally are limited, and commentaries devoted to single books of the Bible. Commentaries are much more reflective of the author's personality and theology, and there are different types of commentaries, depending on what you're looking for as you study God's Word.

Critical, technical, and exegetical commentaries are the most detailed. They exhaustively go through the details, commenting on the Hebrew, Aramaic, and Greek words of the text. They are perhaps most helpful to people who are students of the biblical languages. An example of this type of commentary is *Meyer's Commentary*, a twenty-one-volume set written in the nineteenth century by the German theologian and pastor, Heinrich August Wilhelm Meyer.

Expository commentaries are written to help people who regularly teach or preach from Scripture, though they are very helpful for any serious student of the Bible. They go passage-by-passage, and sometimes sentence-by-sentence, explaining the background and meaning. The real value in these commentaries is that they often go one step further by describing how the meaning of the text may be applied in real life. A helpful example here would be *The Bible Exposition Commentary* in six volumes by Warren Wiersbe.

Devotional commentaries spend little time on the details of biblical passages and instead go straight to spiritual meaning and life application. My favorite one of these is Matthew Henry's commentary. You may find his language outdated at times, but give him time; he'll grow on you. Matthew Henry had an amazing ability to extract every helpful ounce of Bible out of the text and apply it to life. I find myself turning to this commentary quite often in my personal Bible study and for my preaching.

DISCUSSION QUESTIONS

Chapter 1 – What Just Happened?

1. Read 2 Corinthians 5:17 and Ezekiel 36:26. Explain in your own words what it means to be a "new creation."

2. At the moment of your salvation, you received the Holy Spirit (Ephesians 1:13-14). Read the following verses and discuss what the Holy Spirit does: John 14:26, Romans 8:26-27, Romans 15:13, Titus 3:5, Galatians 5:16-18, Ephesians 5:18, and 1 Corinthians 12:4.

3. Explore the following verses to further understand your new identity in Christ: Genesis 1:27, Psalm 139:1-14, Matthew 10:29-31, Ephesians 2:8, 1 John 3:1, 1 John 1:9, Philippians 3:20, Romans 4:5, and 1 Peter 2:9-10.

Chapter 2 – Assurance: How to Know That You Know

1. Do you have any doubts that you are saved? How can you examine your heart to determine that you truly gave your life to Christ? Read through the questions on page 11 and settle the matter.

2. What does the Bible have to say about losing your salvation? See John 10:28-29.

3. How should you deal with doubts? Are there any benefits to doubt? What Bible verses can help you with your doubts?

4. When Christ comes into your life, He brings *new* with Him. As you read through the chapter, which "new thing" was the most impactful to you personally? Which "new thing" are you hoping to experience?

Chapter 3 – Baptism: The Waters of Obedience

1. Do you view baptism as an act of obedience? Why do you choose to obey God? Is it out of fear? Are you looking for a reward? Or are you simply obeying because you love Him?

2. Read Colossians 3. How can you relate these verses to baptism? Explain the symbolism shown in "taking off the old" and "putting on the new" in relation to baptism.

3. How are salvation and baptism different? Can you have one without the other? How are they related?

4. Have you been baptized as a believer in Christ? If not, are you willing to publicly proclaim that you have repented and asked Jesus Christ to be the Lord of your life?

5. What next step do you need to take to be baptized?

Chapter 4 – The Lord's Supper: A Celebration of Mankind's Deliverance

1. Read the Passover story in Exodus 11 through Exodus 12:14. In Luke 22:7-20, Jesus led His disciples in the first communion at the Passover meal

in Jerusalem. With His death and resurrection, we now remember His blood as the ultimate payment for our sins. How did Jesus transform Passover into the Lord's Supper, and what was the new covenant He made with believers?

2. How can you partake in the Lord's Supper and "do this in remembrance of Me"? What are you remembering?

3. Read 1 Corinthians 11:27-34. What are the ways you can come to the Table of the Lord in an unworthy manner (with wrong motives)? How should you approach the Table?

Chapter 5 – Connecting: How Do You Relate to the Church?

1. In Matthew 16, Jesus asked His disciples, "Who do you say that I am?" Can you answer that same question? If someone stopped you walking down the street, what would you tell them about Jesus?

2. Read Acts 2:41-47. What was the response of those who heard Peter's message and were saved? What are some ways that you can respond to the message of Jesus and find community in the local church?

3. According to the Great Commandment (Matthew 22:36-40) and the Great Commission (Matthew 28:16-20), what are the five purposes of a believer? Are you living out these faith components? What can you do to make this a part of your life?

4. Do you understand and believe the importance of local church membership? Are you ready to be obedient to God and become a member of a local church? Read 1 Corinthians 12:12-27 and discuss

how all the members play a role in the
church body.

5. What next step can you take toward becoming a
    church member?

Chapter 6 – Spiritual Maturity: Growing as a Follower of Jesus

1. What are some steps that you need to take today to
    awaken intimacy with God?

2. Whether you are a morning person or not, can you
    start your day with worship? Why is this
    so important?

3. Write down a few reminders that you are loved
    by God. Here are a few verses to get you started:
    Psalm 139:1-4, 13-14, 1 Corinthians 7:23, 1 John
    3:1, Romans 6:10, 2 Corinthians 5:17, Isaiah 54:10.

4. Will you commit to reading your Bible daily? Start
    in The Gospel of John for just a few minutes
    each day.

5. Consider prayers as a conversation between you
    and God. Can you start talking to Him today?
    Are you willing to open up to Him and reveal
    your thoughts, hurts, cares, and plans? He already
    knows them, and He wants His child (that's you!)
    to talk with Him about them.

Chapter 7 – Giving: The Sermon on the Amount

1. Paul wrote in 1 Timothy 6:10 that "the love of
    money is at the root of all kinds of evil." Money
    is not necessarily the issue; it's the love of it. It is
    about our attitude towards money. Examine your
    heart and determine your attitude towards money.
    Does your attitude line up with Scripture?

2. Read 1 Timothy 6:6-8 and discuss what Paul is teaching about contentment. (Also read Philippians 4:11-12 for Paul's personal testimony regarding money and contentment.)

3. The way you hold on to your money can signify a trust issue with God. In Matthew 6:25-34, God reminds us that He takes care of the birds and the flowers, and we are more valuable to Him than both. Do you worry about money? How can you begin to turn this area over to the Lord and trust Him with your needs?

4. How should you give? Do you see a need and meet it? Are you responding to God's command to give? Are you a "cheerful giver"? (2 Corinthians 9:7)

Chapter 8 – Quiet Time: Being Alone with God

1. What is the key principle in this chapter? What do you feel that the Lord was highlighting to you?

2. How do you intentionally connect with God through a daily quiet time? What does that look like?

3. Reflect on the following statement: "Spending time with God is not meant to be a burden." What hinders Christians from having a daily quiet time?

4. For many, time is the biggest hindrance keeping them from having a daily quiet time. What can you remove or rearrange to add time with God to your schedule?

5. For further study, read: Psalm 119, Mark 1:35, and James 4:8-10.

6. Pray a prayer of commitment to God to have a daily quiet time with Him every day this week.

Chapter 9 – Prayer: Communicating with God

1. What do you pray most for? What are you reluctant to pray about?

2. Read Matthew 7:7-12. What does Jesus say about bringing your requests to Him?

3. Think about the prayers you have seen God answer. How does that affect how you pray now?

4. Read and reflect on Philippians 1:9-11.

5. What specific requests are weighing on your heart right now? Commit to praying for those specific things throughout the week.

Chapter 10 – Sharing Your Faith: Telling Others about Christ

1. What are some key moments in your life where you have seen God at work?

2. What fears do you have about sharing your testimony? What fears do you have about sharing your faith with others? What does Jesus say about these fears?

3. The focus of the Great Commission (Matthew 28:16-20) is making disciples. What is a disciple? How are you fulfilling the Great Commission?

4. How can you, today, begin being a missionary for Christ?

5. For a more in-depth study, this week read: Mark 16:14-16, Luke 24:45-49, John 20:19-23, and Acts 1.

6. Work on writing down parts of your testimony this week. Journal about how different events have affected the course of your life and where you have seen God at work.

IN APPRECIATION

I n the end, when the writing must be done, a writer ends up being a loner. Nobody else but he or she is left to do it. But on the way to arriving at that point, many helping hands have given a boost, and thanks are in order.

My thanks begin with my Lord and Savior Jesus Christ. I have never gotten over Your gracious gift of salvation to me.

I thank my parents, Ned and Joan Cranston, who raised me to love God, the Bible, and His Church. Dad passed away during the time I was writing this book, and he has now realized the blessed hope of every follower of Christ: to see Jesus face to face.

My in-laws, John and Gerry Woodward—for your unending encouragement, unceasing belief in me, and consistent prayer support.

My wife and children—Darlene, Tiffany, Lauren, and Emily—you truly inspire and motivate me. Thanks for encouraging me throughout the writing process. The book would have likely been completed sooner had we not made numerous trips to Atlanta and the South Carolina

Upstate to visit you all and the other little blessings God has brought into our lives: Callie, Cade, Colton, and Charley. Thanks also to our sons-in-law, Bryan Coker, Ryan Kelly, and Devin Solberg for being wonderful husbands to my daughters.

My deep appreciation also goes out to . . .

Dr. John Hull and Brian Jones—who are wonderful brothers in ministry. You two have never met, but you both have helped me steer the course, kept me in the game, and encouraged me that this book needed to be written. And you kept me laughing along the way.

Donna Brooks—for taking my thoughts and scribblings and using your literary expertise to turn them into something that we hope will help many, many people.

Andrea Smith—for using your creativity to make *Your Greatest Adventure* attractive on the outside.

Lauren Kelly—for casting the deciding vote on the book title.

Emily Solberg—You are a fantastic photographer. Thank you for the beautiful cover photo.

Sharon Hull—for your inventiveness in suggesting book titles, one of which we landed on.

Tiffany Coker and Liz Lucarini—As "Team Cranston" you both proved invaluable to me. I wouldn't know what I was doing or where I was going most of the time without your able assistance. Thanks for all of your help in research, riding herd on datelines and deadlines, writing the discussion questions, and pushing this project through to the end.

Paul and Margaret Norris—You generously provided me with an incredible setting in the North Carolina mountains in which to write much of this book. I've fallen in love with that view of Whiteside Mountain. Thank you.

Dr. Geoff Pound and Michael Dalton—Thank you for your vision to start and maintain John Broadbanks Publishing and for encouraging me to start, maintain, and finish *Your Greatest Adventure*.

Jason Best and the LowCountry Community Church Elder Board—Thank you, men, for granting me the time to write this book. We have seen thousands turn to Jesus over the years, and I know it is our combined prayer that God will strengthen new believers through *Your Greatest Adventure*. Jason, Bill Clark, Brad Tholen, Kevin Farruggio, Erac Priester, Mark Wease, Marcellus Bonner, Jim Cutler, Kevin Owens—it's been a delight and joy serving God alongside of you.

ABOUT THE AUTHOR

Since 1999, Jeff Cranston has served as the lead pastor of LowCountry Community Church (LCC), an innovative faith community in Bluffton, South Carolina. In 2013 and 2014, LCC was named by *Outreach Magazine* as one of the 100 Fastest-Growing Churches in America, and today more than 2,500 people call LCC their spiritual home each week.

Jeff is a graduate of Columbia International University (B.S.) and Moody Theological Seminary (M.A.). He has served in leadership positions in churches and parachurch organizations for more than thirty-five years.

Jeff is the author of *What Christians Need to Know About Islam* (2005) and *Happily Ever After: Studies in the Beatitudes* (2010). He loves being a father of three married daughters and grandfather to four wonderful grandchildren. Jeff has been married to his college sweetheart, Darlene, for more than thirty-five years.

NOTES

A Convert's First Prayer

1 *Valley of Vision.* Edited by Arthur Bennett. (Edinburgh: Banner of Truth Trust, 1975), pp. 94-95.

Preface

1 John F. MacArthur, Jr., *Keys to Spiritual Growth.* (Old Tappan, New Jersey: Fleming H. Revell Company, 1976), p. 10.

By Way of Introduction

1 C. S. Lewis, *Mere Christianity.* (New York: Macmillan, 1952), p. 161.

2 Matthew 13:3-9 (NLT)

3 A parable was a distinctive teaching method employed by Jesus using everyday things His hearers would readily grasp. Through comparison and story, He used earthly examples to convey kingdom of God principles.

4 Psalms 14:1 (ESV)

5 Matthew 13:19 (ESV)

6 Matthew 13:20-21 (ESV)

7 Matthew 13:22 (ESV)

8 Matthew 13:23 (ESV)

9 Luke 8:15 (ESV)

10 William Cowper, *William Cowper's Olney Hymns,* from Cowper's poems. (New York: Sheldon and Company).

Chapter One – What Just Happened?

1 C. H. Spurgeon. Metropolitan Tabernacle Pulpit, "Every Man's Necessity." No. 1455. A sermon delivered by C. H. Spurgeon at the Metropolitan Tabernacle, Newington, England. January 1879.

2 2 Corinthians 5:17 (NASB)

3 "Futile Renovations," Bible.org, accessed December 28, 2019, https://bible.org/illustration/futile-renovations

4 Galatians 2:20 (NASB)

5 Ezekiel 36:26 (NASB)

6 John C. Maxwell, *One Hour with God.* (El Cajon, California: INJOY, 1994).

7 Matthew 10:39 (GWT)

8 2 Corinthians 8:11 (NASB)

Chapter Two – Assurance: How to Know That You Know

1 *Anne of Green Gables: The Musical,* script by Don Harron, music by Norman Campbell, lyrics by Don Harron, Norman Campbell, Elaine Campbell, and Mavor Moore, based on the book by L. M. Montgomery, Boston: L. C. Page & Company, 1908.

2 2 Corinthians 13:5 (MSG)

3 Hebrews 6:8 (NIV)

4 John 10:27-29 (NLT)

5 John 5:24 (NIV)

6 Gene Kranz, *Failure is Not an Option,* (New York: Simon & Schuster Paperbacks, 2000), pp. 200-201.

7 1 John 5:12-13 (MSG)

8 Psalm 66:18 (MSG)

9 Philippians 2:13 (NCV)

10 Romans 9:21 (NIV)

11 Proverbs 3:5-6 (NIV)

12 2 Corinthians 5:17 (MSG)

13 New International Version

14 John 17:3 (NJB)

15 Luke 24:32 (TLB)

16 1 John 2:27 (NIV)

17 Lord Byron, *Poetry of Byron, Chosen and Arranged by Matthew Arnold*, (London: Macmillan and Co., 1881; Bartleby.com, 2013).

18 1 John 3:14 (NCV)

19 John 21:16b (MSG)

20 John 20:28 (NIV)

21 Luke 7:20 (MSG)

Chapter Three – Baptism: The Waters of Obedience

1 Murphy's Law: If anything can go wrong, it will.

2 Matthew 28:18-20 (NIV)

3 Chronological Life Application Study Bible, New Living Translation. (Carol Stream, Illinois: Tyndale House Publishers, 2012), p. 562.

4 John 14:15 (NASB)

5 John 7:17 (NIV)

6 1 Samuel 15:22 (KJV)

7 James 2:10 (NASB)

8 David Shibley, *The Missions Addiction: Capturing God's Passion for the World*, (Lake Mary, Florida: Charisma House, 2001).

9 Mark 16:15-16 (NLT)

10 1 Corinthians 15:3 (MSG)

11 Acts 4:12 (NLT)

12 Matthew 28:19a (NIV)

13 *The Baptist Magazine for 1830.* Volume XXII, Vol. V, Third Series. (London: George Wightman, 24, Paternoster Row, 1830), pp. 547-549.

14 Acts 8:38-39a (NIV)

15 Mark 16:16 (NLT)

16 Acts 8:36 (NIV)

17 Acts 2:38 (MSG)

18 Acts 10:47 (MSG)

19 Romans 8:16 (GW)

20 Rick Warren, *The Purpose Driven Life: What On Earth Am I Here For?* (Grand Rapids, Michigan: Zondervan, 2002), p. 121.

Chapter Four – The Lord's Supper: A Celebration of Mankind's Deliverance

1 "The History," Concord Grape Association, accessed November 24, 2019, http://www.concordgrape.org/bodyhistory.html

2 1 Corinthians 11:17-34 (NIV)

3 Luke 22:20 (NASB)

4 "Pliny, Letters 10.96-97," Georgetown University, accessed October 18, 2019. http://faculty.georgetown.edu/jod/texts/pliny.html

5 Acts 2:42 (MSG)

6 1 Corinthians 1:10 (NLT)

7 1 Corinthians 3:1 (NCV)

8 John MacArthur, *1 Corinthians: The MacArthur New Testament Commentaries.* (Chicago: Moody Publishers: 1984).

9 Matthew 13:25 (KJV)

10 Acts 5:29 (MSG)

11 Titus 3:10 (NLT)

12 1 Corinthians 11:25 (MSG)

13 Matthew 26:30 (KJV)

14 1 Thessalonians 4:17 (NIV)

15 Romans 5:8 (NJB)

16 1 Corinthians 11:27 (TLB)

17 Romans 8:1 (CEV)

18 1 Corinthians 11:30 (MSG)

19 Acts 5:3 (NIV)

20 1 John 1:9 (TLB)

21 Richard Innis, "Leonardo Da Vinci's Cup," *The Christian Post*, accessed September 15, 2019, https://www.christianpost.com/news/leonardo-da-vinci-s-cup.html

Chapter Five – Connecting: How Do You Relate to the Church?

1 Julian Huxley, *Religion without Revelation*, (New York: Harper & Bros., 1957).

2 Matthew 16:13-16 (NLT)

3 Matthew 16:16 (ESV)

4 C. S. Lewis and Walter Hooper. *God in the Dock: Essays on Theology and Ethics*, (United Kingdom: Eerdmans, 1970).

5 Acts 2:42-47 (NLT)

6 Matthew 28:18-20 (NASB)

7 Matthew 22:35-40 (NASB)

8 Luis Bush, "The Meaning of ethne in Matthew 20:18," Joshua Project, accessed May 8, 2019. https://joshua-project.net/assets/media/articles/meaning-of-ethne-in-matthew.pdf

9 Matthew 16:18 (MSG)

10 Rick Warren, *The Purpose Driven Life: What On Earth Am I Here For?* (Zondervan: Grand Rapids, Michigan, 2002), p. 132.

11 Ephesians 2:19 (TLB)

Chapter Six – Spiritual Maturity: Growing as a Follower of Jesus

1 Mark 1:35 (NASB)

2 Deuteronomy 4:39 (NIV)

3 Psalm 31:21a (HCSB)

4 Psalm 119:11 (NLT)

5 Psalm 119:105 (NLT)

6 "Should I use a paraphrase of the Bible?" Got Questions Ministries, accessed July 9, 2019, https://www.gotquestions.org/paraphrase-Bible.html

7 Matthew 11:28, 30 (NIV)

8 Psalm 119:165 (NCV)

9 Bill Hybels, *Too Busy Not to Pray*. (Downers Grove: Intervarsity Press, 1988), p. 13.

10 2 Peter 3:18 (NASB)

Chapter Seven – Giving: The Sermon on the Amount

1 Charles Dickens, *Oliver Twist*. (Ware [England]: Wordsworth Editions, 2000).

2 Ecclesiastes 5:10-11 (NIV)

3 Ibid. (TLB)

4 Matthew 19:23 (MSG)

5 1 Timothy 6:10 (NLT)

6 1 Timothy 6:6-10 (MSG)

7 Hebrews 13:5 (NKJV)

8 1 Timothy 6:9 (GW)

9 Psalm 50:10 (KJV)

10 1 Timothy 6:9 (GW)

11 Matthew 6:24 (TLB)

12 Proverbs 30:8-9a (MSG)

13 Job 31:24-25, 28 (TLB)

14 Proverbs 11:28 (TLB)

15 1 Timothy 6:17-19 (NASB)

16 "C. T. Studd – Missionary to Africa, China and India," Missions Box, accessed November 24, 2019, https://missionsbox.org/missionary-bio/ct-studd/

17 "Moody Bible Institute," Moody Bible Institute, accessed November 24, 2019, https://www.moody.edu/about

18 Mark 4:19 (NIV)

19 Matthew 6:33 (NIV)

20 New International Version

21 English Standard Version

22 Holman Christian Standard Bible

23 New International Version

24 Malachi 3:8 (NASB)

25 1 John 3:17 (NIV)

26 New International Version

27 Acts 11:27-29 (NIV)

28 2 Corinthians 9:7a (NIV)

29 1 Corinthians 16:2a (NIV)

30 2 Corinthians 8:2 (NIV)

31 2 Corinthians 8:7 (NIV)

32 Matthew 6:3 (NIV)

33 New International Version

Chapter Eight – Quiet Time: Being Alone with God

1 Bryan Chapell, *Christ-Centered Preaching: Redeeming the Expository Sermon*, Second edition. (Grand Rapids, Michigan: Baker Books, 2005), p. 289.

2 John 5:39 (NIV)

3 Luke 18:9-24 (NLT)

4 A. B. Simpson, "Himself," *Hymns of the Christian Life*, No. 2, A. B. Simpson, May Agnew Stephens, Louise

Shepard, Frank J. Metcalf, (New York: Christian Alliance Publishing Co., Old Orchard Convention, 1897), #376.

5 1 Thessalonians 5:16-18 (NASB)

6 Philippians 4:6-7 (NASB)

7 Psalm 1:2 (NASB)

8 *Today in the Word*, Moody Bible Institute, (Chicago: Moody Publishing, June 29, 1992).

Chapter Nine – Prayer: Communicating with God

1 Lionel B. Fletcher, *After Conversion – What?* (London: Marshall, Morgan and Scott, Ltd. 1936), p. 51.

2 Isaiah 31:5 (CEV)

3 Matthew 6:9 (NASB)

4 "The Lord's Prayer" quoted throughout this chapter is from Matthew 6:9-14 (NASB)

5 Psalm 103:13 (NLT)

6 Luke 4:18-19

7 Revelation 11:15

8 "epiousios," Blue Letter Bible, Accessed October 20, 2019, https://www.blueletterbible.org/lang/Lexicon/Lexicon. cfm?strongs=G1967&t=NASB

9 New International Version

10 Dwight L. Moody, *Prevailing Prayer*, Moody Bible Institute, (Chicago: Moody Publishing, 2016).

11 New International Version

12 Romans 8:28 (NKJV)

13 Garth Brooks, "Unanswered Prayers," recorded 1989-1990, track 7 on *No Fences*, Capital Nashville, August 1990, compact disc.

14 1 Thessalonians 5:17 (NASB)

Chapter Ten – Sharing Your Faith: Telling Others about Christ

1 Natalie Babbitt, *The Search for Delicious*, (New York: Farrar, Straus and Giroux, 1969).

2 John 6:35 (NASB)

3 Psalm 34:8 (NASB)

4 Matthew 28:19-20 (NASB)

5 Acts 22:1-3 (NIV)

6 Acts 22:4-5 (NIV)

7 Acts 22:6-10 (NIV)

8 Acts 22:11-16 (NIV)

9 1 Peter 3:15 (NIV)

10 "The Sinking of the Dorchester," Ministry 127, accessed February 19, 2019, https://www.ministry127.com/resources/illustration/the-sinking-of-the-dorchester

BIBLE TRANSLATIONS

Contemporary English Version: Scripture quotations marked CEV are from the Contemporary English Version, Copyright © 1991, 1992, 1995 by American Bible Society. Used by Permission.

English Standard Version: Scripture quotations marked ESV are from The ESV® Bible (The Holy Bible, English Standard Version®), copyright © 2001 by Crossway, a publishing ministry of Good News Publishers. Used by permission. All rights reserved.

God's Word Translation: Scripture quotations marked GW are taken from GOD'S WORD®, © 1995, God's Word to the Nations. Used by permission of God's Word Mission Society.

Holman Christian Standard Bible: Scripture quotations marked HCSB are taken from the Holman Christian Standard Bible®, Copyright © 1999, 2000, 2002, 2003, 2009 by Holman Bible Publishers. Used by permission. Holman Christian Standard Bible®, Holman CSB®, and HCSB® are federally registered trademarks of Holman Bible Publishers.

King James Version: Scripture quotations marked KJV are taken from the King James Version, which is in the public domain in the United States.

The Living Bible: Scripture quotations marked TLB are taken from The Living Bible copyright © 1971 by Tyndale House Foundation. Used by permission of Tyndale House Publishers Inc., Carol Stream, Illinois 60188. All rights reserved. The Living Bible, TLB, and The Living Bible logo are registered trademarks of Tyndale House Publishers.

Made in the USA
Columbia, SC
20 September 2020

20312212R00098